THE ME I FOUND

a journey

margie belrose

All proceeds from the sales of this book benefit
The Belrose Performing Arts Center Scholarship Fund.

The Belrose Performing Arts Center
is a 501(c)3 non-profit organization.
California organization No. 94-2736124

This Book is Dedicated
To my two cherished children, Davy and Dea.

To the beautiful and talented Davida Wills Herwin
who inspired 'the me' and insisted my play and now this book be written.

To Sue Sue Finegan a true and loyal friend for over forty years.

To Robert Micheli who began his training here at eleven years old becoming my
first complete apprentice learning every aspect of The Belrose.
Upon graduating, I suggested he find a conservatory for the performing arts
rather than a university. Robert is now a working actor in New York,
having earned an Equity card.

I wish to express a special thank you to my daughters partner
Joanne Wishart who went far and above the call of duty in searching for many
hours, looking thru over 1,000 images to get just the right one for the book cover.

Also to Kim Huff for her dedication in making my efforts worthwhile
in the final editing of this book.

I would also like to give my gratitude and appreciation to Lelia Elliott
who has stood by me even when the tears of frustration would not stop.

I wish to especially thank the technical and editorial volunteer staff
with expertise, for their unselfish help thru these several years:
Ann Groven, Nicole Gostnell, Debby and Mike Ziegenhagen
Kaitlin Chin, and Charlene Eldon.

INTRODUCTION
As We Stroll Forward

Scene by scene, by scene, this unrelenting
compulsion to write my story, has been an
emotional struggle for many full moons.
My adult life has often been one of the never-ending joy
of dancing, singing, acting, performing, teaching,
"So why this urgent need to now write? Don't know."
"What will the end result be?"

Perhaps a novel, an autobiography, a series of essays, a narrative, a memoir, a philosophy of my life, or all of the above jumbled together?

I'll just attempt to write with all my healthy heart that is almost beating out of my restless body, Will I be dumbfounded at what the surprise ending will be? Yep and it is sure to be a surprise.

I am not a writer in the truest sense, as you will surely see, although I have written several plays in recent years, collaborated in many of our original plays and revues, as well as the lyrics to thirty-one songs. Some will be within these pages, and then it will be joyfully shouted out, the end.

"Oh dear, is Margie Belrose ready to challenge this formidable project?"

The decision is to not concern myself with punctuation, or pure grammar (I leave that to the proficiency of others). Accomplished writers do it easily and beautifully. That said just know intriguing words that are hard to pronounce, and exquisite sounding French quotes (that I don't even know, and wish I did) will not be included, as this book is not intended to be the offering of a literary gift.

However I will keep at my right hand side, the two dog eared books of education that will be delved into when needed: the thesaurus and dictionary.

Yes, this person attempting to write this story, is vulnerable, even petrified of embracing such a mammoth task, when there are many thousands of gifted writers now, in the past, and who will come hereafter? I will approach my delicate efforts tentatively.

All writers, in any venue, humble 'the me' as my concerted effort with each word and thought will be to absorb from them. But still I must write what I believe to be the truth and what is in this pulsating heart of mine.

An unusual form of courage is urging me on. Is it hidden within 'the me' and will my ineptitude be forgiven?

The trust is that the story of my unusual life will speak for itself, without any bells or whistles, even to be significant, in some infinitesimal way with the subliminal purpose of tenderly affecting your life.

Various titles have buzzed around in my muddled head for a number of months, perhaps:

"The Saga of Margie B,"
"Margie Belrose — Her Story,"
"Stuff Happens... and Then,"
"The Diary of Margie Belrose,"
Well now maybe... Aha, "The Me I Found."
So, you do see what became my ongoing dilemma?

My tumultuous life has been unconventional, as you will quickly surmise. Therefore this eager attempt at writing will follow in that same dipsy fashion. Some writers have advised:

"Write what you know, what you believe to be the truth."

Obviously for 'me' that can be the only course to set my unsure feet on.

The blight of my young life, with its scattered and many confusing memories, holds a stubborn ache to revisit some now blurred events of a childhood that blindly skirted 'me' by.

Not knowing the absolute truth in some scenes of my knotty story, various segments will turn out to be what surely are rational and believable to 'the me'.

For vague reasons that I do not know and may never comprehend, this swerving venture is vital to 'the me' as I approach the September years of my still young life.

My friend Charlie, a published and gifted writer, (and a very nice man) suggested: "Try to infuse your story here and there with a sense of humor, Margie. You know, be funny when possible."

"This I will work on Charlie, as soon as I discover how to unring the bell."

THERE ARE JOURNEYS

Lyrics by Margie Belrose

Dedicated to my life

THERE ARE JOURNEYS AHEAD OF ME
UPS AND DOWNS AND GETAWAYS
TROUBLES I CAN'T YET FORESEE
TO THE NORTH, SOUTH, WEST AND EAST
TO THE UPS AND DOWNS THAT WILL FOLLOW ME
I WILL LAUGH, I WILL CRY, I WILL BE SCARED
PERHAPS I WILL DIE
I GUESS IT'S CALLED THE JOURNEY OF LIFE
BUT THINGS WILL HAPPEN
NO MATTER HOW I TRY
SOME FULL OF FUN, SADNESS AND STRIFE
I WILL TAKE EACH STEP AS I MUST DO
TO WALK THIS BUMPY JOURNEY OF LIFE

© 2009 Margie Belrose

Begin at the beginning
said the King in Alice in Wonderland,
go til you come to the end,
then stop.

On this particular day, perhaps a lazy daisy day, that you have chosen to kick back and pick up this particular book to read or just peruse, I invite you to stroll with 'the me'. We will mosey hand-in-hand, for the next few hours, as each scene of my convoluted life unfolds.

During our stroll we will sometimes veer left, then right, maybe even go backwards at times, but it is not possible to saunter in a logical straight line.

So, per chance, you will grasp why there are many deviations. This is important for you to remember so that somehow my life's story will make sense.

With our fertile imaginations let's conjure up scores of adventures together. Sometime the happy ups in my adulthood, as well as the sad downs in my childhood.

The emancipated trust is that you will feel the forgiving sorrows deep in your own hearts. Possibly you will savor the unexpected smells of an unfamiliar culture, hear the beautiful sounds of a world not yet known to you. You may experience my exuberant and sometimes terrible emotions of an existence still striving to reveal its' avenue of life, to find 'the me' at last.

No doubt you will be aware of warm tears tumbling out of your sparkling eyes. This surprise happened to 'me', in writing such a fragmented saga.

With tenderness I brushed them away so I could be aware of joy and laughter. Therefore my understanding friend, we will now take hands and stroll to the first scene. We can call it:

Act I
SCENE ONE

Not having been born yet, it can only be imagined how the long, uncertain, and even dangerous, journey from Greece to America was for the three inexperienced teenagers.

The youngest, Sophie, would very quickly, in her burgeoning youth, bring 'the me', with normal excruciating childbirth pain, into the whirling world of confusion, fear and wonder.

The three eager youngsters, all much too anxious to grow up, were taking their one and only trip of youthful adventure to the unfeasible. They chose to venture on an old ocean liner that would toss about in the wild fury of the magnificent and challenging Atlantic Ocean. The bulky wooden boat was creaking in her earnest effort to reach Ellis Island. More than three hundred exhausted and apprehensive immigrants were aboard, that had travelled from many corners of the globe to reach the miracle of all miracles.

The weather turned into a misty and chilly evening before their highly anticipated New York arrival. The small trio was snuggled in their secret hiding nook on the wet and slick upper deck. They were trying to help their older brother John from getting sicker below deck.

Suddenly, John, jumped up, scrambling to the ship's railing, his two sisters rushed after him, loudly begging: "John, please don't jump, don't jump."

His color had now become pea-green, throwing up what he could, although they had not eaten for two days. Hearing their urgent pleas, he managed; with slow and dizzying caution, to turn around, looking by now white as new fallen snow. In their instant relief they began to laugh and cry simultaneously.

Stumbling back to their dim hideaway under a stepladder to the lower deck, they hugged each other, although they were completely exhausted and drifted off to sleep in each other's arms.

As early dawn awakened the three sleepy heads, the over-burdened ship was unusually still and quiet. Suddenly to their surprise they heard some excitable laughter.

While rubbing the sleep out of their squinting eyes, they moved curiously to the side of the liner that they were so very anxious to leave.

A multitude of people were milling around on the ground below, waving large hand-printed signs in the early morning New York breeze.

The animated throngs were shouting happy greetings to their loved ones and friends still on board.

It was difficult for the excited family of three to discern the messages on the scores of wind-swept signs in their enthusiastic searching, but it did not take them long to recognize one sign bobbing up and down. It was hardly decipherable, but did read "Vasilakis." "That's us, that's us! Hurry, come on, let's collect our stuff and get off the ship."

With their hearts racing, and with little patience, they scrambled off the boat that had been their unsavory temporary home. They ran crazily to this stranger who shared their name. Of course they had, with jittery nerves, be officially cleared before leaving the island. A nice looking stranger, with a quiet demeanor, introduced himself: "I think I am your Uncle Peter."

Peter had been told that three unknown relatives would be arriving from the homeland of his ancestors, which he had left more than two decades before.

In their blissful relief at finally setting foot on the welcoming American soil, they were unable to stop their endless chattering while scrambling to a rickety machine Peter called a car. The teens simply stopped, in their tracks, almost tripping Peter, while staring in disbelief at the oddity. They had never seen such a peculiar contraption in their hometown of Greece, their beloved birthplace, which they were already missing dearly.

With uncontrollable giggles, they grabbed their things and jammed into Peter's quaint piece of equipment with great curiosity and mild trepidation.

Uncle Peter, with restrained, but unusual happiness, haltingly explains: "We will go to my little house in Brooklyn where you will meet many Greek families and friends. It isn't far from here."

Their eyes blinked very wide, as this fascinating world of usurping mystery astonished them with every turn of Peters steering wheel. They could not help but gawk at what was unfolding before their adolescent eyes. It was undeniably too much to soak up and take in.

Their tummies began rumbling when they neared a Greek settlement that seemed so surprisingly familiar, at the same time, enveloping them with odd sadness.

Such a warm touch of Greece began to settle over them and brought with it an unswerving twinge for their home they left such a short time ago and would never forget.

Within minutes, their attention was riveted to the wonderful pungent smell of lamb, bread and other Greek delicacies that filled the breezy air and made them dizzy with ravenous hunger.

At last they sat down in Peter's attractive home to a festive Greek meal prepared by Peter's wife, Olga. They experienced again the same tender memory for their childhood home thousands of miles away. The teenagers had yet to realize they would never again travel back to their distant place of birth.

With wise wisdom, Peter announced to his tired and anxious relatives:

"You can rest here for a few days to catch your breath. Then we can pack up your belongings in my automobile and be off to nearby Long Branch, New Jersey, not far from here. You will have the opportunity to meet other relatives and new friends.

There will be work for you John, in this glorious territory called America. A land I fell hopelessly in love with when arriving here, over twenty years ago, as an adventurous man your age."

The three uninformed foreigners were dreadfully disheartened not to find the streets lined with glistening gold.

This was a myth that had been perpetrated many times by other soon-to-be disappointed, but equally innocent travelers. Even so, they continued to rummage thru the byways and the roughly paved roads for such a wondrous phenomenon.

In their curious wonderings they would, in due course, discover this new world had many avenues to be wary of. But what did it matter? They were delirious, and felt this was a thrilling paradise full of promise; a bridge to the never-ending wonders of a continuous and incredible discovery.

The interest of unforeseen adventures tempted them to bashfully experience everything they were hungrily craving to garner, in this new exciting life before them.

In an amazingly brief period of time, the intelligent threesome began to speak and understand the difficult language they heard everywhere, albeit, spoken in colorful broken English.

The young greenhorns were frantic to spread their fledgling wings in separate directions, but not until they shared many tearful goodbyes and thank you's.

John traveled the short distance with his Uncle Peter to Brooklyn. On their way Peter modestly offered him work in his small but thriving fruit and vegetable store. The polite young boy was then invited to share Peter and Olga's modest home. They had no children of their own.

Violet, the second oldest, with childlike excitement, boarded a tourist bus that was headed for the buzzing beach town of Asbury Park, New Jersey. She heard it was a thrilling and alive small metropolis, with the beautiful, ever-changing Atlantic Ocean as the exquisite background.

In no time she met an older, sophisticated Greek restaurateur who spotted her as she flirtingly sauntered down the squeaky wooden boardwalk. Without realizing it, she entered a fast and impulsive marriage and they, all too soon, started their family. Violet may have had regrets but there was no turning back as her life course was permanently set.

Sophie was invited to live temporally with her generous cousin, Irene. They spent many days romping and playing in Long Branch. Sophie soon wondered off alone, probing every nook and cranny for her share of life's many gifts.

She was an attractive young girl and knew whatever drifted into her inquisitive direction would be hers alone and special.

After a few months, she unabashedly learned to foist her charms on everyone she met in this hard to believe, celebrated world of amazing sights.

Sophie was a fairly accomplished swimmer and during one of her daily joy-seeking excursions throughout the small town, she randomly found the local outdoor swimming pool. With childish excitement she skipped the short distance to swim every day.

On an unusually humid afternoon, while sunbathing in her skimpy blue bathing suit, she began flirting outrageously with a dashing older Greek man, John Leonides. With no vacillation, he more than willingly exchanged her shameless advances.

In Sophie's raw unsophisticated years of only fifteen, she could not know that this mysterious handsome man would and could become dangerously belligerent after imbibing only a few tempting drinks of wine.

Sophie would hit upon this cruel personality trait in him only after their quick, passionate and irresponsible marriage in the ominous year of 1927.

In the blink of an eye it became evident that he would never change the chronic drinking habit that he had acquired as a young lad of twelve in his birthplace of Samos, Greece.

He was powerless to amend his debilitating habit for her, or for the children he would soon recklessly father. John could not alter his lifelong destructive pattern for anyone or anything, nor did he want to.

John Leonides was an unswerving addict, causing him to become helplessly violent in ways Sophie never imagined. This horrific and dark transformation in John's personality would fill her with disquiet consternation every miserable day, even hour of her three-year tormented marriage.

The couple barely knew each other when they exchanged vows of forever love. Sophie had just reached a youthful amusement-seeking sixteen years of age. John was an experienced man ten years her senior, and with sly manipulative charm, swept her off her tiny feet and into her still innocent mind.

By the year of 1929, they brought two pretty girls, Ethel and Margarete into a world wracked by the crushing global depression.

Nonetheless it would seem to an onlooker, that an ideal life was at their beck and call in spite of the appalling worldly conditions. They were of the same ethnic origin, speaking their beautiful Greek language; their lives were seemingly laid out before them.

However, in no time they would prove themselves to be a selfish, match for match pair.

For many months Sophie premeditated a terrifying escape from her unpredictable husband. She had by now acquired an ardent Greek lover, Harry. In view of their thoughtless and brief affair, and because there was no consideration of the disastrous consequences, a bastard child was on the way.

Harry was not the handsome man her disparaging husband was, and though his demeanor was a quiet and mushy meek, she instantaneously knew he would comply with her constant demure demands with nary a murmur. She held the firm belief he would make a dependable 'second' husband, unlike the near monster she thoughtlessly wedded.

Harry had never known a woman, or rather someone who was not yet a woman, like Sophie. Without shilly-shallying, he became obsessed and obedient to her ever incessant, beguiling, and often wicked demands.

Her second pink cherub had been delivered out of her womb at a moment in time when she held the staunch idea that she was madly in love with her husband, a stranger really. This emotion was all too soon erased out of Sophie's quickly changing persona.

It is hard to imagine her surprising vehement words to the astonished nurse on the early morning of the delivery of her new daughter. Her body was still oozing the after birth warm blood, as she frantically uttered while rolling to her side: "Take that thing away, and the other one too. They were terrible mistakes, I don't want them, they are a horrible part of John. Give them away they are nothing to me not now, or ever will be. Get this new thing out of my sight."

Sophie watched in disbelief as John had all too soon begun to descend into pure evil. Each day she tried fruitlessly to recognize such a chameleon of a horror, as the man she vowed, "I do" with.

By now she could only discern that he was no longer the charming man with whom she had so quickly and rakishly become enamored. This fearful man had now turned into a bleak, somber eternity of incredible proportions.

Looking at him through her once bright blue eyes, there was not a smidgen in his whole being that could be described as attractive or desirable, but just the unholy opposite. John's lifetime of alcohol consumption now began, almost overnight, to rapidly permeate every cell of this once attractive, educated and intelligent man.

For Sophie, the reality of their future together was forever and irretrievably a vanishing fabrication of her undeveloped imagination.

Much of John's ghastly actions were far beyond sinful. When he became verbally abusive, without warning he would spin into unexpected brutal physical violence. This was an observed pattern Sophie would soon imitate and take on and into her own unbecoming personalities.

In time she would discover he was also a dishonest man. On occasion in asking with great trepidation, where his money came from, in a fit of anger, he would not reveal the truth of the matter or how they would pay their mounting expenses.

She had no inner qualms in believing that her disparaging husband was a lifetime functioning alcoholic, a compulsive gambler, and a chain smoker. He had proven this many times over. He forever stank of bad garlic, cigarettes and stale wine. These revolting bodily odors seemed to come out of his very pores. Such repugnancies were the abhorrent and stomach-turning qualities the young bride found out only too soon into their short, ill-fated union.

To flee from her violent and unsavory life with him forever was the only refuge she doubtlessly and justly felt she had to take.

Her escape was methodically planned for many anxious months with her lover. Now on this early, summer morning, in July of 1930, Sophie was in the turbulent throws of making her terrifying life-change become a certainty and a definite reality with her devoted lover at her side.

She had to run away from such a place of cruelty and near insanity, as she saw it and precariously lived it every day.

Ironically in a brief time the same evil persona would overtake and consume her own undeveloped character.

John was what he was, and no kind miracle from the blue heavens above, would ever transform him.

Sophie had terrible traits also, and was far from the lily-white young girl he had impetuously married. Despite her deceitful resolve at being otherwise, she was rather audacious with a mean, almost cruel streak on the ready rise, in her undefined development.

On rare occasions when John appeared somewhat sober, he failed to recognize that his wife could be just as selfish, self-absorbed, cruel and irresponsible, as was his nature.

John's young child-bride spent her days vicariously living the lives of the numerous complicated characters she compulsively read about in the piles of trashy romance magazines she cleverly hid from her husband. This along with secretly hiding her smoking addiction, or so she thought. Sophie was not perceptive enough to recognize the unpleasant stench hung everywhere, in her clothes, hair and in the atmosphere of her surroundings that eventually trickled out of her own pores.

Her immature behavior and fixated escape became totally obsessive, even to the obvious neglect of her little ones. They cried incessantly while lying in their wet cribs screaming to be fed, cleaned and held.

Such an unfortunate, shadowy, alliance was predestined in a more than dreadful shattering manner. Therefore, the unsympathetic abandonment of her new young family would have severe consequences that would blaze forever into the soon to be abandoned, neglected and unloved human beings. The pitiless woman who recklessly tossed them away perpetrated this sad and dark doom. The desertion began at the hour of their births.

In her heart of hearts, Sophie was unable to find even a modicum of affection for her offspring; could not ever, could not hold with loving arms, could not reach out with kisses, and cuddly hugs while cooing tender baby talk into their delicate ears. It was as if they had not been delivered out of her youthful body, but out of another's, not hers, and thus she gave them not a thought or care.

Sophie slept fitfully that dark night in an urgent complex anticipation, in the now hateful bed she had shared with a man she no longer loved and found impossible to even like.

It was beyond this urgency that she rise early and quietly, to set in motion her fearless escape, and in all honesty, her utterly self-serving betrayal.

She felt her heart throbbing loud and fast. The grave dread that John would wake up from his nightly drunken stupor caused her body to tremble with overpowering trepidation. He then might hear that same throbbing nearly bursting out of her delicate body along with the quiet sobs she valiantly struggled to stifle. If so, he could easily erupt into his customary, uncontrollable violence.

It took less than twenty-four months of incredible terror of both physical and verbal abuse from John for young Sophie to realize she could no longer abide the never-ending, volatile and dangerous life with her manic partner.

She silently scurried about with frenzied impatience on that warm July morning, gathering a few necessities for the newly arrived babies she would never feel love for, not ever, but only hate.

On this never to be forgotten summer morning, the tiny brood most surely had been reminding Sophie, for many months, of the despicable man she had so often made passionate love to, but now came to despise and continually avoid.

Her feelings of suffocating disgust for fearsome John unquestionably spilled into the same hateful emotions that with no concern or thought, she ruthlessly projected onto her undeserving newborns.

Sophie, with quickening haste, her body hardly able to keep up with unbelievable and uncontrolled anxiety, finally and cautiously fled her sparsely furnished cottage. With unbelievable fear she quietly closed the door behind her for all time, running swiftly and breathlessly into the arms of her passionate and feeble coconspirator, Harry Gallos.

Though on the brink of becoming a womanly woman, she prematurely discovered her strength in a myriad of behaviors.

Therefore, not surprisingly, her delectable sexual deeds and needs became the open, tantalizing and irresistible bait she blatantly offered.

Hopeless and weak Harry willingly obeyed everything she shrewdly demanded, without faltering. He was totally defenseless under her influential sexual power, and would always pander to her self-centered and very often destructive evil biddings. It mattered not to him her conniving motives, as his own sexual passions drove him further and further into an unholy abyss.

He took total protective custody of his mistress as he waited patiently for his nightly reward, which was always there to salaciously devour him.

Twenty-eight-year-old Harry was under the blinding sway of this undeveloped girl. She did not have to be summoned to be at his side as he could not resist her total abandonment. Therefore he ignorantly aided her on that unforgettable and formidable morning in their self-centered plan to desert two unsuspecting babies for all time.

Sophie and Harry never glanced back or gave thought to their dishonorable betrayal of the innocent lives of two new human beings. But their alliance ultimately revealed itself to be an unforgiving and despicable union. Their lack of conscious was lots more than a wicked sin.

SCENE TWO

The giant antique town clock in the city square of Long Branch struck sharply at six a.m. on that muggy July morning when the callous couple drove up to an unknown childcare center.

Sophie all but fell out of Harry's car, in her young and foolish exhilaration to escape her miserable life.

She was now holding the delicate one-year-old, Margarete, whiles her slightly bigger two-year-old Ethel stumbled behind. Ethel was barely able to carry the oversized paper bag of supplies and was trying oh so hard, with child-like effort, to keep up with the rash and impatient, soon to be a long gone mother.

Sophie was now yelling above the occasional horns of the early morning traffic, "Hurry up, hurry up, you measly brat."

Unable to stop crying, Ethel tripped on the uneven sidewalk skinning both knees. When the pathetic supplies tumbled out of the large sack, Sophie spun around and smacked her across the head. She then grabbed Ethel's skinny arm, and maliciously forced the sobbing child to gather up the meager things by her injured self.

Unconcerned, Sophie brashly ignored the wretched mishap, continuing to prod and push the ill-treated and screaming tot toward the door of the nursery. This could only be described as cold-hearted and atrocious behavior.

The middle-aged attendant witnessed the heartbreaking scene of brutality, so with extra gentle affection and loving care, she swooped up the toddlers, trying to sooth the inconsolable Ethel. The soon to be absent mother, above the resounding noise, yelled out: "I will return for them at six." She knew full well there was no intention of returning at the promised time, or ever.

Sophie, in her foolhardy and juvenile conduct, was on an irrational highway to an imagined fantasy and freedom from her tireless daily responsibilities. She sought to possibly explore another life of exciting adventure.

Sophie did not comprehended as yet, that this new life of expectations with Harry would unquestionably dish up the same every day dull obligations she was now seriously trying to escape from. Without thought, she was soon to deliver another possibly unwanted child.

The attendant had to wait until well past six thirty, when she had to call for the children's inebriated father. No doubt Sophie had filled out a form with his number on it.

After several hours of a speedy and experienced search by the local police, the devious teenager was found hiding in the lobby of a nearby cheap hotel with her zealous lover and equally cruel and self-effacing servant. The conniving young mother was immediately arrested for the abandonment of her offspring, and sent to a woman's prison. Soon after, John vindictively obtained an uncontested divorce.

The irregular and self-consumed pair, John and Sophie, never saw each other again as far as can be determined. However, the hate they exuded toward one another never dissipated through the years, and was dispassionately held forever in their blackish of hearts.

Harry's daughter, named Frances, was born during Sophie's well-deserved incarceration. When irreverently released, Sophie and Harry joined forces to begin a long self-absorbed life, with its own familiar obligatory responsibilities staring them in the face from that day on.

These very motherly duties were exactly what Sophie was desperately trying to escape from. She imagined her new life with Harry would be the absolute opposite of her life with John, minus the constant abuse. Eventually, they brought into the world their own son, ironically named John.

Sophie never made even a futile attempt to find the sweet harmless children she gave birth to when she was but a child herself. However, through a set of future abysmal circumstances, she would, with unrelenting resentment, vile hatred, and consumed brutality, abandon them several times over. This will be sadly revealed as we continue to trod this dithering potholed and often cheerless road together.

"It will end up happy, I promise. Continue to stroll with 'me'."

"Did Sophie nakedly spew out her loathing and burning vengeance on her two blameless victims?" Undoubtedly her calamitous deeds of evil, was the outcome of the identical horrid emotions she felt towards John. This is just hard conjecture, but seemingly can be thought to be the utter, bitter and irrefutable fact.

After Sophie's arrest, irresponsible John Leonides was obliviously ignorant of how to care for his little charges: how to love them, change their diapers or even how and what to feed them.

He cleverly fabricated stories to tell unsuspecting acquaintances willing to listen "My wife is very sick. She is in a wheelchair. She is in the hospital. My wife is dead. I'm alone with no one to look after my young babies."

Most often people felt immense sorrow for the befuddled man. They helped where they could, never realizing the truth, and naively believing the deceptions that came out of the two-sided mouth of such a cunning man.

For years, my sister Ethel believed that a person she called mother was in a place she named heaven, and would often weep despondently over her perceived loss.

This absurd belief was hers alone, and was not ever possible for 'me' to believe, entertain or accept. Therefore, I never did. "Ethel, I don't think this person you call 'mother' is dead or in heaven. Besides, what is dead? Where is this place called heaven anyway? What do you know? You're lying. Why do you lie all the time? What is this person's name? And what is a mother? I don't believe anything you say. Why do you make up stories?"

Deep down the knowledge was always there, that 'the me' was never to recapture or experience for the rest of my years the same complete safety, warmth and protection, I tenaciously clung to while growing for nine warm months in the belly of a woman who would deliver 'me' suddenly into a cold world. She did give 'me' life, only to then be abandoned with no compunctions, at my tender one year of age.

My sheltered haven had been to cuddle my yet to be formed body and to serenely nestle up all those many months, in my very own special, quiet, dim, moist, warm, and loving pouch.

SCENE THREE

My first discernible memory is not of a loving person with adoration holding 'the me', but rather as a little three-year-old, (I think), dancing and skipping on a grassy lawn, somewhere in the world – twirling around and around in a flimsy yellow butterfly dress while singing, "I'm going to be a dancer, I'm going to be a dancer." "Where did this magic word 'dancer' that would forever more reach into my life come from? And where did I ever see a dancer? I just don't know."

But this remembrance is as clear now as if I'm still there, at this very moment: "joyfully living such a magical afternoon, an afternoon that would for all time, shape my life and become a constant and never changing dream."

On that lovely day of whirling playfully around, it was to be the very first flicker of a fantasy, of my all time aspiration that never changed. And that is what I became, first and foremost: A DANCER.

It was to be the foundation and solid rock of 'the me' I was helpless to stop looking for. The 'me' that has involuntarily persisted in attempting to achieve my elusive dream. No matter the ups and downs, the in's, the out's, the turns left or right, the good, the bad, the fears, or the apprehensions. Even my silly follies now and then did not deter me from my flight of imagination.

Most importantly, the peeking through of a conceivably safe refuge for happiness coming from somewhere, and from someone that would enfold 'the me' in protective and loving arms. The 'search' and the 'dream' was all that mattered and became the very spirit and personification of my life for all time.

In my memory searching for remembrances, once, when strapped in a wooden highchair with a towel, to hold 'me' in, a tall, dark-haired lady with long red fingernails slapped 'me' hard across the face: "was this unimportant baby, 'me' crying? Maybe I didn't want to eat? Or maybe I wanted to? Maybe I needed a wet diaper to be changed? Or perchance I just wanted to be held close to someone's soft, warm and inviting breast?"

It had been raining hard and relentlessly for several days and the streets were filling up with swirling water. When the rain finally stopped: "Oh what fun it is to splash around in the high gutter." But with horror, an emotion I had never felt before, I fell screaming and slipped into the rain filled gutter, even though it had seemed so inviting just a few moments before. But now I began sliding, sliding, oh-so-quickly toward the beckoning dirty sewer.

By some chance, a big bush was there and I grabbed onto it with my tiny hands to save myself. This was possibly my first bump into a cold, wet death: "The sad ending of a little darling that no one would even know of, miss, want or care about."

Oops here is another just-found memory. During an obscure afternoon, there was a rather large toy silver metal airplane on the ground, so of course with child-like delight, I picked it up to sit on pretending to fly." I'm flying, up, up I go, wheee, oh what fun, where to go?"

Then in my three-year-old uncontainable glee, a large branch on the ground suddenly tripped 'me'. My left eye was painfully cut by one of the sharp wings. Warm red blood spurted out everywhere: "Who took 'me' to the hospital? Who was the lady that slapped 'me' and why? Did it all happen on the same day?" Of course, I never knew. Have a small scar to remind 'me' of such a remembered and anxious filled day.

Another almost forgotten, time, we were in Boston, (I think), and while happily bouncing an oversized ball in the middle of a busy horn-blowing street, I cried while falling to the bumpy cobblestone street. Then a large green truck loomed toward 'me' but stopped just short. My second skirmish with death. "Why was 'the me' in Boston?"

These are just a few of my earliest memories, not yet a three-year-old, and there are a few more to follow as we travel this zigzagging stroll together.

Don't forget as we stroll, we might veer left, right, forward, even backward. If you can remember this, my story might then have some intelligent meaning.

There is no memory of being loved, held, kissed, cuddled, or looking up into someone's kind face, smiling and tickling 'the me'. But how could this person called, 'me' know what was missing in such a 'cast-off life', then and sadly forevermore?

About the same time, somewhere in my peculiar life of uncertainty, darkness seemed to suddenly surround us. Hundreds of people were in a lot of cold water almost up to their necks. My sister screamed: "We're in a flood."

"What is a flood, Ethel, and where did all this water come from? I'm scared, look how fast the cold water is coming toward us, oh, and I'm slipping under the water, help. Where is Papa? Help, somebody!"

Lots of men in small boats were frantically paddling up and down the flooded streets, in their heroic, but near to useless attempts to rescue all the terrified and screaming people.

My older sister tried to yank 'me' through the water, the best she could with her young arms, but the slippery brown mud dragged 'me' down anyway. I began to spiral over and over into the shivering racing water. "Help, my sister is drowning, help, help, someone, please come and help her."

It is a wonder that swimming was always fun and part of my juvenile years, even earning 'me' a 'swimmer's badge' at fifteen years old.

A burly man, rowing one of the bobbing boats, quickly reached down, gathering 'me' up and out of the frightening water: "Here little one let me wrap my jacket around you."

"I'm so cold, my breath won't come."

A little diversion please.

How do we remember some things clearly, all the details, and others not at all? For instance: "Never went to a dentist till nineteen years old. Don't remember brushing my teeth. They should all be rotten, but aren't. Who taught me anything at all? Who trained the little 'me' how to tie my shoes, how to go to the bathroom or comb my hair? Who took care of my frequent bloody and scabby knees and elbows? Who gave me a bath and washed my hair? Did I ever go to a doctor? Who taught 'me' to read and write and have polite manners and show respect?"

Back to our stroll.

The big, brave man with a bushy beard stopped the rowboat, dropping the wooden paddles in front of the glass doors of a very large building that must have been a school. Our fearless rescuer helped us out of the boat:

"Thank you, sir, for saving 'me,' but I still can't catch my breath." He gently patted my back. "Hear the gurgling sounds? That means you'll be just fine now, take your sister's hand, and hurry into that building. Bye-bye, don't cry, you're safe for now."

People were lying down wherever they could find a bit of room, on the shiny but wet floor. Blankets and coats were warming them as they huddled closely together and were just as scared as we both were. I heard soft sobs and some screams, coming from all corners of the very large room, while parents and friends of the trembling children were cuddling and comforting them.

People kept rushing with their nerves on edge, to the big doors while searching, with fear in their eyes and dread in their hearts, as they desperately looked for their missing loved ones, maybe even their own children.

There is no likely way to know when this unforgettable night of pure panic and fear ended or even where we were in a spinning world that would, for many years, bring inconceivable terror into our lives. "Ethel, where is Papa, do you think he fell in the water? Who are these people, and where are they taking us? I'm scared, hold 'me', and don't pull so hard, that hurts."

This, then, was my third encounter with death that always seemed to be mysteriously lurking and niggling about, ready to capture the unwary and timid 'me'.

About this time in my upside-down existence, we were on a dairy farm somewhere. A farmer lifted 'me' onto a pretty brown pony. Then boom, fell off, and into a cow (you know what). The farmer picked the stinky 'me' up and (yuck) cleaned 'me'. He was used to that smell.

He also grew potatoes on his farm, showing us how to dig for them, which was a lot of fun, even though we were quickly covered with wet dirt. Later in the day, when he cleaned us up again, he offered us some buttermilk. "Oh dear, how awful the strange lumpy drink tasted."

My father suddenly appeared out of nowhere. He gruffly announced to his two bewildered girls: "We are going to York today, to the home of a Greek family, that are having an important celebration."

When entering the crowded house, I heard people laughing and talking in a language that was weird and also wonderful to listen to. An exceptionally handsome Greek priest insisted: "Come with me, Margarete, to the upstairs porch where there is a little bird's nest, you will like them they are so cute."

When getting to the top of the wooden landing, he crept up behind 'me', pushing his body towards 'me' very hard. Somehow knew this was wrong, even though my age wasn't more than four. I squirmed away from his reach and ran down the stairs, out of breath, to the lady whose house we were in. I kept pulling on her hand, unable to explain anything. She tousled the hair of this fretful child, giving lots of hugs, but then scooted 'me' off with a gentle pat.

This was the end of such an unusual day, which came out of nowhere, and from my memory, rather like a dream, but not.

About my sweet age of four (I think) my father, who insisted we call him Papa, although we rarely saw him, cause many different people watched over us, I think.

We stepped on a big bus that took us to a scary big brick building in Detroit, Michigan. "Where are we going Papa, what is this place called? Where are we going? Are you coming back? I don't want to be here. Are you leaving us again, are we bad?"

"It is called The Protestant Home and Asylum. You will live here for now. I don't know when I will be back. Goodbye."

He brusquely turned and left us, screaming after him: "What is an asylum papa, why are we here, are you ever coming back, have we been bad again? Are you giving us away?"

Once again we were left alone, and it seemed we lived in a state of perpetual bewilderment, with strangers, always strangers; some were nice and others, well. "Ethel, are you scared too? Where are you going, don't leave, hold my hand, this place is giving 'me' the shivers, will they hurt us here too?"

My solitary confusing memory is of being deserted in a terrifying dark big building. Children were running everywhere, laughing, some of them crying and yelling, others fighting, some hiding under furniture.

The two frazzled attendants were in a craze trying to catch the rambunctious children who were relentlessly teasing them as they scampered about playing games of tag, and hiding. 'The me' was sure this was a place to be scared of.

A tiny child, much like myself, was sitting by herself on the end of a bench in a corner, all curled up and alone. She was rocking while hugging herself, with no clothes on. This precious blond child was quietly making sounds as she sucked on her tiny thumb. Slowly I walked over to her, taking my blue, worn out sweater off, wrapped it around the little naked, bird-like toddler. It was only natural to snuggle up next to her, give her a hug and begin to suck my thumb with the same slurping sounds. Something I never did before or after.

Oh gosh, remembering this is all so clear, and tells 'the me' to shed a few forgotten tears. There is no memory of ever seeing that dear young soul again. Most of the time the helpers were kind and this asylum did not turn out to have many creepy things happen, except that something was wrong with 'me'. Children often chased 'me', with torments, as they sing-songed: "You're crazy, you're crazy, Margaret is crazy."

Before going to bed each night we had to stand in line fidgeting not wanting to swallow the nightly spoon of unpleasant cod liver oil. "This is good for you. Close your eyes, now don't make that face."

Often, we sat down to eat pudding at night and hot cereal in the morning. This food was almost always lumpy or burnt, or both. One morning, suddenly feeling very sick after such a breakfast, I threw up all over others and myself.

To this day cannot eat, or smell, hot cereal or pudding. Once, a girl skipped over teasing: "Let's play doctor." She grabbed my hand, swinging 'me' around and laughing. Don't know if we ever did play doctor. Kind grey haired ladies would come at times and give every "crazy orphan" an orange. Loved chewing the peels, even to this day.

SCENE FOUR

Shortly after our dubious entrance into this "asylum" we were whisked off to another big place reeking of a terrible stench. A little cherubic lady wearing a long white dress and cute hat put us to bed then covered our puzzled faces with a washcloth that had the same sickening smell as the building. "Let 'me' out, I don't want to be here. What are you doing? I don't want to go to sleep, let 'me' up."

"Your adenoids and tonsils have been taken out."

"What were they used for, were they bad? Please let 'me' see them and have them back. Miss nurse, thank you for the ice cream. May I get up now, please?"

When we were to leave that noontime, from such a strange big building with the overpowering smell, they gave each of us a bowl of chocolate pudding. "Here, little one, sit down and eat this before you leave, it will make you feel better." I never liked chocolate pudding as you have been told so when the nurse left, I shyly tried to find a place to dump it. Looking out the window: "Hmm, maybe down there? Can't, we are up two stories and people are walking everywhere. What if this pukey stuff plopped on someone's head?"

Lifting up the clean white pillow, there went the wiggly brown gunk. When discovering such a disgusting mess, "What did that poor nurse think of such a naughty child? Shame, shame."

Soon a man drove up in a yellow car with black stripes, to drive us back to "the home." "Did we live in the Protestant Asylum for over two years? Just don't know, but think so maybe even three."

At my young age, time was formless and indistinct. Never knew where we were or when. Thus, this story may appear discombobulated. "But this was already explained as a possibility, right?"

Without warning, and probably a few years after being taken to the hospital, Papa stormed, really fuming, into the weird asylum. This was to be another day that would carry more doses of well-known fear. At seeing the two of us, he immediately smacked us on our heads, for no reason. We began to quietly sob, of course. "I'll bet at least four gallons or more of salty tears fell out of my blue eyes in those early years and the years thereafter in my mystifying life."

Maybe we reminded this loathsome stranger named John of a period in his life that he could not forget- a time when we were brought into his strange realm of uncertainty.

He pushed us out the big front doors. Papa was out of control, angry, loud, and spouting mean words to everyone: "Get out of my way, you bi***" As always there was no talking to us, maybe because we were too young to understand. But still there was no explaining of anything, just pushing, cursing, slapping, and causing us to cry all the time. Of course, he stunk like a lot of unpleasant things. "Was he really slapping and cursing Sophie in his misplaced anger and delusion?"

We couldn't sit close enough in our dreaded silence. Then papa, with uncalled-for malice, shoved us with another mean whack into a roaring, smelly bus. Ethel tripped on the first step getting into the unsightly bus that was to cart us off to somewhere we could only envision would bring us more fear and tears. We fell over each other; no one cared or offered to help. A loud voice hoarsely announced:

"Those of you headed for Saginaw, get on board. We're leaving now. Hurry up people, we're on a time schedule, hurry up."

When we stepped off the deafening bus, we began to walk, for what surely were blocks and blocks, then boom, we were dumped, unceremoniously, into the unusual carved doors of St. Vincent's Orphanage and Asylum, in Saginaw. The sight of a big dark brick structure had now become familiar in a formidable way. This strange building turned out to be yet another asylum for us to be carelessly discarded in.

We were hastily forsaken and duly forgotten for over three unhappy and panic filled years by the man that was our father. The slipshod disposal of us by the two egotistical humanoids who gave us the start of a sketchy life was only the fearful beginning of an existence of desertion that scarred the two of us, albeit quite differently, for all time.

We were petrified of the solemn faced ladies, gliding confidently in their slow pace, wearing big, white, very stiff, wing-like, things on their heads, no hair was showing. Everything was serene, no sounds could be heard, and the air appeared hazy.

"Let 'me' play with my sister. Where is she? Why are you pulling on 'me'? Let go of my arm. Are you going to hurt us here too? Where is my sister? Where did my Papa go? When is he coming back? He isn't coming back, is he, cause he doesn't want us? He doesn't love us. Is he is giving us away again?"

Ethel refused to make friends. Several times in her life, even as an adult, she would confide: "I'm not going to like them before they have a chance to not like me, and I just know they won't, cause no one ever likes me. I'll show them."

Consequently, she never gave anyone a fair opening, and certainly not to herself. This self-destructive cynical attitude of hers would all too soon become the insidious style of her distraught nature.

So often she did not want something LIKE you had, she wanted WHAT you had. She cleverly found devious, thieving ways to abscond with what she wanted, at any cost, even mine, being her mere hint of a sister.

Her life seemed to appallingly overflow with deep-seated hurt, which was for her, no doubt, indescribable. Her forlorn empty days were glumly consumed with envy, sorrow, jealousy, and total lonesomeness. This was unmistakably evident in the despair of Ethel, and it hurt 'me' to my very core. This older sister of mine remained for all time incredibly complicated and always tough to understand.

She subsequently could not help but become progressively more hostile with each passing moment of her tormented years. The never-ending, near to evil down ward twisting of her despondency began when we were inoffensively innocent and so often forsaken. Unbelievably, it happened more to her than 'me'. This strange phenomenon cannot be explained or explored psychologically and has been a curious question asked of myself over the years, with never an apt answer.

On that grave day of being abruptly planted in St. Vincent's Orphanage, we both began to visibly shake. "Go sit on that wooden bench in the hall." This said to us in a severe tone as we looked out tiny windows onto a play yard, where no children were playing.

One of the disquieting ladies, with the identical huge white headdress, slowly glided over to us holding towels that smelled so awful we tried to hold our noses. She then gave each of us an under served slap, without saying a word while wrapping what she called kerosene, smelly towels around our heads. "What are lice? Besides my head doesn't itch. Where do they come from?" Children walked by, poking nasty laughing fun. Through my stinging tears: "Why are you laughing? And besides, there are no lice in my hair, so there. Bet this happened to you too. Go away."

On our first full day at St. Vincent's, Sister Regina, the Mother Superior, was found dead in her sacred cubicle. Later 'The me' peeked in, when no one was looking, and saw a narrow bed, dresser, chair, and crucifix that barely filled the sparse space.

I did not know what this 'dead' meant. She was laid out in the small anteroom. Everyone was quietly sobbing, and in my bewilderment, not ever seeing the head nun before, no tears would come even as I stared at the still body of a person that could not be acknowledged by 'me'. "What does dead mean anyway? Ethel who are these ladies in their long black and white uniforms?"

"They are nuns, the Sisters of Charity, and are angels. We are going to that far away place called heaven."

Through my utter disbelief and confusion: "I won't go, I won't go. You can't make 'me'."

"Yes you will. Now get on your knees and start to pray. You have to pray because we're going to be with our mother soon."

"That's not true. You're always lying. How do you know? Besides, why do I have to get on my knees and what does praying mean? What good would that do anyway? Does it hurt? You keep saying mother, what does mother mean? Besides you don't know what you're talking about, you're lying again. I don't like you even a little bit when you lie. Why do you tell lies?"

It took only a few days for a skinny nun, Sister Mary Matthew, to look at us and to dislike us intensely. This sister with a mean frown had a rather large nose that could honestly be described as 'ugly'. "Maybe she didn't like us because we weren't Catholic. Who's to know?"

Very soon, with no explanations ever, the "good" servant of God, delivered torments often and in many forms. Hundreds of whacks with a wooden ruler, anywhere and anytime she felt like it on our frail, still very insignificant bodies. Once her vicious ruler split in half over my bony back, at which point the kind' Sister Theresa ushered 'the me' to bed for over a week:

Bed was a cozy and safe place to nestle into. It was a welcome escape where there were no punishments or unkind words viciously taunted at 'me'.

Often for many hours, our strict discipline was to kneel upright under a big piano. I still have a little bump on each of my knees. I don't recall ever hearing anyone play the pretty brown piano. To wile away the frequent hours of deprivation, my fingers would trace over the beautiful carvings of the piano legs while quietly singing to myself a song taught by Sister Theresa: "Jesus loves me yes I know cause the bible tells me so."

Another one of the unnerving penalties heartlessly heaped on 'me' was to stand, very still, facing a stark white wall with hands clasped behind my back. It became very painful, as I was not permitted to lean on anything. Sister Mary Matthew, with sheer malice, and abrasively instructing 'me' to stare straight ahead, with no blinking, for what must have been a long time. As said, time was very vague.

Once, when I was unable to stand up, I crumbled to the floor in a dizzy spell. Sister then deemed another hard mean hit with her new ruler was well deserved on this little orphan called 'the me'.

"Was this person really so naughty?" She gave another violent kick with her foot; wearing her clumsy black shoes. She tried to wake 'me' and then shuffled 'me' off to bed, weeping, with no supper. There is no memory of doing "bad things." "What was 'bad' anyway? I didn't understand."

We were time and again deprived of the evening play hour. I was ordered to go to my specified bed before dark. It became part of the dreaded sister's daily assault. When first seeing the movie "The Wizard of Oz", it was instantly apparent: "The wicked witch had to be fashioned exactly after the wicked Sister Mary Matthew. They were without a doubt, one and the same."

Our memories of being callously treated have never completely absented themselves from either one of us, to infinite and varying degrees: "Don't think about that nasty Sister. Ethel please just don't. This will all be over some day when we are older. You'll see- we can't be here forever. Did you know Phyllis just turned eighteen and is leaving soon? Don't cry. At least for now we have a place to live, to eat, to sleep, and be warm, lets hold each other, try to be happy. Wanna play?"

"Who was the older sibling?"

But no matter the disappointing encouragements I innocently served up, the daily tortures, remained in Ethel's forlorn memory even till her last breath on earth. They so overburdened her she was unable to confront the bottomless veils of ugly evils for what they were. She appeared to be unable to even begin to recognize the neurotic sicknesses of the monsters that unfairly dealt them out blow-by-blow, day-by-day and for years. As a consequence she, in turn, unknowingly urbanized the same neurotic sickness. It is what she inadvertently observed, learned and therefore it became her tormented and tortured life. Why 'the me' escaped the same severe emotional burdens cannot be explained.

In today's world, the cruel punishments and deprivations would rightfully be called abuse, and if discovered, my sister and I would have most likely been thrown into the 'system.' "Would that have been better for us? I don't know, but I think not."

The result of such brutal treatment handed out daily, for so long, in the guise of a servant of God, completely destroyed Ethel's frail sense of self-esteem and confidence, and accordingly stripped the essential goodness from her very being forevermore, never to be recovered.

She was mercilessly and maliciously invalidated every day by the 'good' nun's horrendous treatment; far more than 'the me'. "Why not 'me' to the same extent? Maybe because I was smaller and younger. Maybe I wasn't as naughty. Maybe maybe. Whose to know?"

How could Ethel ever know how to be happy and free of overwhelming and undeserved guilt? Often she would agonizingly be over-come with endless sobbing. She was addicted to unmerited self-loathing. "Why is this woman of God so cruel? What horrible things did I do? I must be a very wicked person deserving of never ending punishment."

My all but shattered and perpetually unloved older sister could not stop tormenting herself psychologically. She was trapped with no escape. I don't think she looked for an opening.

Memories for 'the me' are not nearly as devastating, I believe because of the help of my secret spiritual guides I talked to every night.

Most (not all) of my remembrances became manageable and healthy through the years. Some still sear in my most tender place, especially in the early morning hours, when light comes creeping in to shine on 'me'. I then gently push those sad memories out with sustained effort. It has not always been easy, but has become my continued salvation to this day.

In their place at the questioning start of each day, I have substituted thank you's to all the people that have shared love with 'the me' and have come to my aid and rescue, time and time again, my whole life through.

Papa never gave a peek in, even once, to see and check on us during all the neglected years spent in the orphanages and other places that we were placed in. I can barely remember them no matter how hard I've tried.

At some point, my sister and I were almost certain we had no father, and we knew we had no mother. (Of course, we found out later what a mother *** was).

A few children in the 'home' were not all orphans and they had visitors most every Sunday after mass. I could never understand the lengthy masses spoken in Latin, and found myself impatiently unable to stop squirming. "Maybe that was one of the reasons 'the me' was so often punished."

Some of the non-orphan children had parents that brought them weekly 'treats.' Careless children would often throw their orange peels on the ground. I followed them, picked them up, and chewed them. Even though they were gravelly, still, they were treats. Then under tables and chairs, there was gum. Gum I saw kids chomp on and then stick under the furniture when they sucked the entire flavor out, and no one was looking. "A big ball of used gum is now my secret treat. This is my own ball of gum, my own treat. I'll hide it in my very own window seat." That secret ball of gum grew to about the size of a big man's fist. In the wintertime I would place a glass of water outside a nearby window in the freezing cold Michigan morning so it would get icy and crunchy. "My treat alone, that no one knows about."

There were two light brown, slender tiny girls, whose parents came most every week and brought them a box of chocolate covered cherries. Once in awhile, these quiet youngsters would share their bounty with others. I still can remember what those yummies tasted like. "But to this day I never buy them. Possibly because the memories are too hurting for 'the me' to even dimly recall."

The two itty-bitty girls almost sat on top of one another, sucking on their fingers. One had her hand completely turned over, with her pointer and middle fingers stuck in her mouth. The other sucked her thumb and wrapped her index finger over her nose. I tried to do the same thing, but my fingers wouldn't turn the way theirs did, and besides 'me' didn't want to suck my fingers.

Those shy children were very alone and frightened. I never saw anyone talk to them much, not even their parents, who would only stay a short time to visit. I could not talk to them, didn't know how, and 'me' was just as fragile and frightened as they were: "Did those delicious chocolate covered cherries have something to do with my theme song: 'Life Is Just a Bowl of Cherries? Yep."

SCENE FIVE

A digression please.

Early in my freshman year, a girl asked me: "When is your birthday, Margie?"

In my ignorance, I truly did not know what she was talking about, so went to the dean of girls: "Miss Holmes, what is a birthday what does it mean? Do I have one? What is my real age?"

In her astonishment she answered, "Your birthday is July 29th, that is the day you were born and now you are thirteen and a half years old. You will be fourteen in July. Our records show you have no mother and a father that has deserted you and your sister. I'm sorry. Can we help in any way?"

Now back to our stroll.

The only Christmas I was to ever know about until my sweet sixteen, occurred one Christmas morning after six o'clock mass. At this point, I was maybe the age of seven or younger. "How could I have known my age anyway?" I was feeling bashful, watching all the excitement not meant for 'me', as I hesitantly took slow steps into the playroom that had window seats all around for toys and treasures for each child. There was a long white box on part of my very own window seat that was so big it was taking up part of the seat next to mine. "What was this white box doing there? I only had my secret ball of used gum in my window seat that no one knew about. And what was a Christmas anyway?"

Sister Theresa walked over to this awestruck and cheerless child, gently putting her arm around 'me:' "The big box with the pink ribbon is yours, and it's my special Christmas gift to you."

"Could that pink ribbon have anything to do with the color pink being my favorite color, Hmmmm?"

With tears hotly welling up in my blinking eyes: "Oh, no, Sister, it must belong to Evelyn, it's on her window seat too."

"No, it's just for you alone. Here, open it."

With such eager anticipation never known before, the pretty pink bow was hastily but carefully untied: "Oh, what a beautiful baby doll. Is she really mine? Can she sleep with 'me'? We will love each other truly. Little doll of mine, your name is now Theresa." This exceptional doll was to be my only gift of any kind until reaching my life-changing year of sixteen.

Holidays, birthdays, and Sundays have always been a disquieting trauma throughout my life. I have tried sometimes, not always with success, to hide such unforgiving, heartbreaking feelings from my family and others. "Those devastating wounds should be long gone by now, but when the remorseless memories overtake 'me', tears unwillingly leak out of my eyes on those days that are intended for surprises, happiness, love and laughter."

A few days after my joyous, first snowy Christmas, I was foolishly chewing a piece of my gum treats in Sister Mary Matthew's class. She came up behind 'me' and began to hurtfully drag 'me', by my ear, to the front of the surprised class while furiously screaming; "Margaret, you are chewing gum? Where did you get it? Sit on the stool for bad children. You are bad. Put the dunce hat on and stick the gum on the end of your nose." Crying uncontrollably, I tried to do as told, but with shaking hands I accidentally stuck the gum IN my nose.

"Where is the gum? You were told to put it ON your nose."

As I timidly took the gum out of my nose, the scared children laughed nervously, as they were afraid of sister too. She violently yanked me by my scraggly hair, shoving 'me' into an empty classroom. From an old desk drawer, she took out a pair of pointy silver scissors, without saying a word.

This was such unspeakable terror that pulling away from her and crouching down on the floor behind the desk saved 'me' from, what I hoped would be even further untold torture. I naively believed she couldn't reach 'me', but she found a way and pulled 'me' out from under the desk. I cried loudly: "Please, please don't hurt 'me' again. Oh, no, don't cut my hair. A terrible pain goes down to my bottom, please don't, I beg you. Please stop hitting 'me'. I'm sorry I was chewing gum, I never will again."

She chopped my hair off way above my ears. In weeping hysterically, my face was turning red and began to swell up. I covered it and desperately wanted to hide or die, but 'that' Sister hatefully jerked 'me' screaming and kicking back to the grim classroom that was now exceptionally quiet: "Class, doesn't Margaret look better?" No one laughed and to this day, I never ever chew gum and always put off having my hair cut. Nice hair has not been a blessing and I always have it cut short – hate it.

I remember telling the girl who sat next to me in the playroom: "Evelyn, you know what, I think the devil we hear so many terrible things about must have appointed Sister Mary Matthew to be a nun, because God would never hire such a mean, nasty person to be working for him." To be on the good side of Sister, (everyone wanted to be on the 'good side' of her) Evelyn tattled: "No I didn't say that, didn't, didn't."

My dread was so unbearable, I could not remember, at that moment, that such spiteful words came out of my mouth. Of course, I was beaten with near to brutal fierceness everywhere, over and over. The pretty piano by now had become my welcomed second home.

"Think over what terrible things you said, Margaret. You're a bad, bad, girl." I learned a lesson that day: "Be very careful saying unkind things to people about other people. Just don't, don't, don't. Was this an unconscious, though bitter lesson? Yes, it was."

My sister and I were institutionalized in a Catholic orphanage, but we were not of that somber and strict belief. Far back in my memory, there was an afternoon spent somewhere, when I was probably not much older than a year or two, a pool of warm water covered 'me', and I was baptized into the Greek Orthodox faith. No matter. We still had to learn the baffling teachings of the Catholic Church to make what was supposed to be our first confession and communion.

Kind Sister Theresa, very unlike mean Sister Mary Matthew, was often good to 'me'. Once in awhile she would patiently whisper wise words of advice, as she guided 'me' to the side of the small classroom. I never really noticed if she did the same for my sister. No one seemed to take an interest in her, to teach her or to even like her. But then, she didn't want to like anyone either. It was an intricate state of affairs that shrouded everyday of her sad life.

This was to be the course of her incredibly lonely life of despair. Being so little myself, I just didn't know how to help her, make her laugh, how to play or to just sit together. We did not even eat together. In my mind, it seems we hardly saw each other and were kept apart.

After attempting to hopelessly absorb most all the hard-to-grasp teachings and the complex customs of the Catholic religion, Sister Theresa advised us: "You will not be able to go to confession or take communion next week, because you are not Catholic." Calming and instant relief took over my body because no explanation was ever given for what the many punishments were for. "I'm gong to make up some lies to tell the priest at confession and then I will really be naughty," I secretly said this to myself, not knowing what else to confess during the confidential time when I was supposed to talk about the bad things I'd done. Ethel cried and cried: "Please let me take communion and be a Catholic, I'll go to confession and tell father all the bad things I do and think. Please, Please."

In fact, as an adult, she often went to any Catholic church to receive communion, but she never went to confession. Ethel desperately longed to be part of something big and sacred, yearning to be where she would not be overwhelmed with shame of herself and her body. But that blessed relief and sanctity never would share her life. When loving opportunities did filter into her distraught personality, she was compelled, by some inexplicable compulsion, to harshly rebuff them:

"Ethel, all you have to do is try to make friends, and smile at people, then they will like you. Why do you shove everyone away, even 'me'?" Being her slip of a sister, and noticing her despondency develop beyond understanding, I tried over and over to say things that were not even understood by 'me'. Many up side down words scrambled out of my young, and ignorant, mouth in my futile attempt to help her.

SLEEP OFF YOUR BLUES
Lyrics by David and Margie Belrose
Music by Don Deane
Dedicated to my sad and so very
complicated sister

SLEEP OFF YOUR BLUES GOOD NEWS TOMORROW

YOU'LL FIND TONIGHT WAS YESTERDAY

AND WHAT SEEMS BLUE TONIGHT

TOMORROW WON'T SEEM THAT WAY

YOU'LL FIND A KIND TOMORROW IN PLACE

OF LONELY YESTERDAYS

SLEEP OFF YOUR BLUES TONIGHT

TOMORROW'S ANOTHER DAY ANOTHER DAY

YOUR BLUES WILL SOON BE GONE TOMORROW

CAUSE AFTER ALL IT'S JUST ANOTHER DAY

JUST CLOSE YOUR EYES AND ALL YOUR

SORROWS WILL GO AWAY WILL GO AWAY

YOU'LL FIND A KIND TOMORROW IN PLACE

OF LONELY YESTERDAYS

SLEEP OFF YOUR BLUES TONIGHT

TOMORROW'S ANOTHER DAY ANOTHER DAY

SCENE SIX

At approximately six a.m. one exceptionally cold Michigan morning, nine year old Ethel woke up horrified to find that not only her bed clothes, but her whole body was soaked in a pool of her own warm blood: "I know I've been bad, and now God is punishing me. I deserve it. I'm bad, bad, bad." She woke 'me' and we struggled to gather her blood soaked sheets to take them to a small sink. With the determined effort of youth, we tried to wash out the sticky blood that had already stained the white sheets. All the while she could not stop her flood of tears that matched the flood of blood dripping down her young legs. It was not possible for us to scrub the dark blood out before the serious nuns found us.

We were awakened every morning at six a.m. with loud rhythmic clapping by the disciplined nuns. Then sleepily, we would slip out of our warm beds to kneel down, barely able to say or understand the memorized morning prayers. By this time had learned what praying meant but still didn't know how it worked.

On that terror filled day that would paradoxically change Ethel's life forever, Sister Florence found us at the small sink, fruitlessly attempting to wash out the sheets. Water and bright red blood had dripped all over the floor and on us: "Ethel, you are not being naughty. This is your first menstruation. It is normal and is what

every growing girl must go through. All of us have gone thru it too."
It seemed unbelievable to her that even nuns went through the same
bodily change.

Those inept words by Sister Florence were the only useless
explanation given to Ethel. In her frightful confusion: "I don't know
this new word. I'm scared. What is happening to me? I feel very sick,
help me, I'm going to faint. I have awful cramps. I can't stand up.
What shall I do with all this blood coming out of me, Am I dying?
Will it stop, will it happen again?"

There is no memory of anyone cleaning us up or of how the
nuns solved the dilemma of the blood spilling out of Ethel's young
body. She was only an unblemished nine. Though she had been
unfeelingly told she had done nothing wrong, Ethel was convinced
through and through, for years, that she was a dreadful, incorrigible
person, and had to be punished. Ironically she seemed compelled
to do bad things so her firm belief would become true and her
punishment would be well deserved.

After that startling morning, she could not talk to anyone for
days. She sat endlessly in a sullen, bewildered and detached posture,
holding her stomach in an attempt to stifle the non-stop, painful
cramps. She refused to eat. No one consoled her, not a single nun
came to comfort or help her. "Where was kind Sister Theresa? Oh,
Ethel was so alone."

By the time we left the orphanage and later when Ethel
turned fourteen, because of this premature physical change in her
diminutive body, she found ways to be with boys/men on an intimate
level. I knew this when she contracted a disease and needed help.

Again a slight digression.

In today's world of 2010, blatant sexual behavior in boys
and girls who are not yet out of middle school is an unbelievable
common fact. This early unthinking sex-driven behavior is, without

question, robbing many thousands of youngsters today of their rightful childhood innocents.

Back to our stroll.

The result of this alarming transition occurring in my Ethel's early life, with no one to patiently explain about such a terrifying event, it would turn out that what should have been a small problem turned into an agonizing big one. She could not seem to conquer such a devastating experience. It unquestionably altered her physical body and emotional life forever.

With love and understanding during that particular time, her life could have possibly turned into a happy, guilt free existence.

For 'the me', womanhood arrived at a very late fourteen or fifteen and was never to equal the same trauma as my sisters. Years later before my own change, Ethel explained what had happened to her when she was but a withdrawn nine year old: "It was very awful for me, as everything was secretive and hushed. I was embarrassed and ashamed. There was no one to talk to, or help me through, what I now know, as an adult, was a normal womanly change." I remember saying, all those years ago, "Why are you walking and talking in a way I don't recognize? Don't sit with your legs spread so far apart, that isn't nice. Sister will punish you." She was like an unfamiliar person sometimes. Ethel was no longer just a year older than Margie, but much, much older in every way.

Odd that we seldom talked, or became real sisterly buddies.

It was not unusual for the tyrant Sister Mary Matthew to shriek at 'me' in one of her nonstop, oppressive fits of ranting and rage anger: "All of the white things on your fingernails are lies that you have told. One day the heavens will open, fire will come down, the earth will swallow everyone up and you will be responsible for it all." That devastating lie of a horrific story, spun by a woman of God, lived in my gut all during my juvenile years. So often 'the me' would fearfully gaze up at the heavens with anguish expecting devastation to come down upon the world because of 'me'. Creeping under my bed covers became a nightly and stable place to hide and feel safe while holding on, ever so tightly, expecting any minute for the world to come to a destructive end because of 'me'.

In my adult thinking, those white marks on my nails were quite possibly just a vitamin deficiency. Lies never came out of my mouth, not then, not ever. In fact, "Liars are people to be suspicious of, and in time they usually reveal their true pernicious colors."

One warm spring evening in this petrifying place called St. Vincent's, in a cold town called Saginaw, 'The Sister' with no apparent reason, ordered 'me' to bed hours before dark, which happened more often than not. Salty tears would fill my eyes, while hiding again, way under my soft, safe blankets, where there was always refuge and no one could find 'me'.

Sister Theresa came to the side of my bed, and as it would turn out, it became an exceptional night. "You've been a good girl today, come out from under your blankets. Wipe your tears away, there are still a few hours left for you to run about, maybe skate and have fun before dark." This was the first and only time to ever be able to play outside in the warm evening: "here, quickly put on these red and white bloomers so the boys can't look up your dress. Now hurry and go out to the play yard."

We rarely saw boys, because they lived in one wing of the building and the girls in the other. We didn't eat in the same room. All the children (who weren't being punished) were given permission to play games together on Tuesdays and Thursdays.

When I heard that children could live in the asylum until they were eighteen years old, it sent 'me' into a near panic at such an abysmal fact: "Oh gosh, do I have to live here all those years with that awful Sister? My friend Sister Theresa just has to be here to look after 'me'! Sister Mary Matthew makes 'me' itch with hives. Who will take us away when we turn eighteen?"

Often itchy hives spread over my sensitive body that became scaly, and then 'the me', with relief and happiness, would be sent to bed where there was solitude and peace for a few scratchy weeks. Then I didn't have to see or hear the dreaded Sister. Sometimes I would pretend I still had the itchys so bed would console 'me' a little while longer. Writing this book is giving me the same scratchy skin. "Good grief, is 'that person' hovering about?"

That evening when given permission to play outside and have fun was special because: "Margaret you are a good girl."

The happy 'me' skipped outside, and looking around, I felt free in the peaceful evening air taking in some deep sighs. All the while, wondering if my life might one day be safe and happy and with no cruel punishments. Either way, I did not want to skate. Instead, rolling a car tire became my game of fun. Someone yelled out: "Just roll the tire and try to stay with it." Tried and tried.

"Oh, I'm not very good at this. The tire is rolling away."

A blond boy, probably my age, whatever that was, ran after it:

"Wait I'll get it for you, I know how." When he rolled the tire back I put my hand out to stop it. "Thank you, what is your name?" He suddenly and shyly, without looking at 'me', reached down and

tenderly kissed my hand. He kissed my hand. "My name is Carl."
Then he quickly scurried away before the strict nuns would find us
talking.

"Not going to wash my hand ever."

I never set eyes on him again. Up to that point, in my deprived
life of affection, that was my only kiss by anyone. "Oh, to see him
again, to know him. He liked 'me'. Maybe we could become friends."

Phyllis, the oldest girl in the orphanage, was about to be set free
from the home she had hated living in since she was a little child.

She often asked 'me' to run errands and polish her shoes.
I even forced a tic on the left side of my mouth like hers in my
childish admiration of a much older girl. She strummed a guitar and
sometimes invited 'me' to sing along, maybe to pay 'me' back for the
many favors.

One day after school, Sister Theresa guardedly but wisely advised
such a naive child: "You are looking up to Phyllis and want to be like
her and that's not a bad thing, but you must not run her errands
any more, or polish her shoes, and stop doing the same tic on your
mouth like she does. And don't follow her around. She is eighteen
and you are still just a little girl. You are a 'good little girl', be
yourself."

Her words, "be yourself" have wedged deep within 'the me', all
my life. Her kind attention could not help but make 'me' happy
sometimes at St. Vincent's. A home that was duly dreaded but for her
kindness that forever influenced my life. "Margaret, would you like
to lead the rhythm band and learn to play the triangle?"

"Gosh, I must really be a good girl. Why can't Ethel be happy
like this? Why doesn't anyone care about her?"

YOU'RE WORTH IT

Lyrics by Margie Belrose
Dedicated to all neglected and unloved children

I KNOW YOU'RE WORTH IT, I KNOW I'M WORTH IT

GUESS WHAT - - - WE ARE ALL WORTH IT

WE JUST HAVE TO TAKE ONE STEP FORWARD AND THE NEXT

AND THE NEXT TO FIND OUR WORTH, OUR SELF-RESPECT

WHAT ROAD SHALL WE TAKE WE ASK EVERY DAY

PERHAPS IT'S ACADEMIC, OR THE ARTISTIC WAY

MUSIC, DANCE, WRITING, PAINTING

OR MAYBE COMPUTERS – WHAT A WORLD THAT UNFOLDS

ALL THOSE CONVOLUTED ROADS IN OUR SEARCH

IS IT REALLY ENDLESS THIS QUEST TO FIND OUR WORTH

OUR SELF-RESPECT?

BECAUSE YOU'RE WORTH IT, I KNOW I'M WORTH IT

WE'RE ALL WORTH IT IF WE HAVE LEARNED

TO TAKE JUST ONE STEP FORWARD

AND THE NEXT AND NEXT

© Copyright 2009 Margie Belrose

SCENE SEVEN

"Margaret, you are the smartest girl in the second grade. You learned all your multiplications before anyone else and you almost won the spelling bee, except for that one silly word that no one else knew how to spell anyway.

We've determined to have you skip the third grade next year. In two weeks there will be a commencement with our holy bishop coming to perform the ceremony. A rehearsal will be held so your deportment will be proper and it will demonstrate respect for our bishop."

"What does rehearsal mean, Sister Theresa?"

"All of the children receiving an award will be expected to kiss the bishop's ring. He will present each student with a special pin, and you are one of those special children."

To this day a special box holds my special pin that has the word 'excellence' inscribed on it. I still have it, in spite of all the crazy and disruptive years of my life.

Jumping the third grade was a blunder by the nuns and for years I could not catch up in school and never felt smart until my third year of high school.

At the end of the long, somber ceremony, as I hugged my pin, there stood a vaguely familiar figure of a man in the shadows of a faint lit hallway, a person not immediately recognizable. "Oh, maybe he might be my papa, but no, I have no papa."

But it was that man. Hot hysterics quickly flushed over 'me' and I broke into a trembling sweat, staring at the person that would always fill me with fear, a person not seen or heard from in over three years: "How could he be my papa? A crazy orphan is what I am, and that is what I had been told many times." To this day, I think of myself as an orphan. Not crazy, though. "Hmmmm., what do you think, Charlie?"

The strange human standing there did not utter a single sound; rather he simply turned and started to walk away. Hysterically crying out and running towards him: "Look at 'me', Papa. Sister said I was a good girl. Aren't you proud? I'm leading the rhythm band and even know how to play the triangle, see how big I am now. Don't you want 'me'? I won't be any trouble, promise. Don't you love 'me'? Don't you love Ethel? Don't you want us? Are you giving us away again? We won't be bad." There is no memory of my forever-sullen sister or the person called my father actually being at the commencement ceremony.

Papa never looked into my eager tear stained face that evening of my award. "In fact, as 'the me' thinks about it, I realize I never knew the color of his eyes, what his hands looked like or any part of his body, his arms, back, chest or anything. Did he have long or short legs? What was his smile like, and how did his laugh sound? And did he ever laugh?

He never reached to touch 'me' or took my hand or gave fatherly kisses. The only physical memory of him is his thick black hair." I barely remember what his face looked like.

What unloved, abused, and neglected little people we were during all of our young lives, and only because of the narcissistic and self-centered couple who brought us into the whirling world. They indulged in wild and reprehensible acts with no regrets, empathy or well-deserved consequences. The pitiful truth was that we were not wanted or loved by them, and were thrown haphazardly away, just like so much rotten smelly garbage, not once but many times.

"Who were these indescribable people?"

SCENE EIGHT

Each July first, everyone, even the austere nuns, would scramble onto big huffing buses once school was over for the year and the blistery winters of Michigan temporarily disappeared. We were sped off to a special summer camp, giggling and looking forward to undisciplined fun.

I had never seen a swimming pool before, and this camp had a big blue one. There were unpainted yard toys, swings and one slide to play on, and lots of trees to climb.

The trees had strange-looking green and brown insects that looked like sticks, and they scared 'me' on that first day. I ran away from them.

But each day after that, with ever-slow watchfulness, I could not help but search for the unusual insects. Try as I might, I never saw a single one again.

We ate our two daily meals and snacks in a big barn-like room. At night, we eagerly found sleep on narrow cots in the same kind of room, and for eight hours we spent a cozy night's rest. Of course the boys and girls were separated, except for the three hours of afternoon playtime. This summer home some miles from Saginaw was called "Shields Landing", a place to love, play in, be safe and find a bit of willful happiness during the hot and humid summer months.

On Mondays, when we knew the nuns would have their chance to swim, a few petrified but curious kids including 'me' would stealthily creep up and hide behind tall hedges to catch an inquisitive glimpse of them. We were not allowed to swim with them, because it was believed that nuns should only be seen in their full black and white habits .

Their black cotton bathing suits hid every bit of their pure bodies; even their hair was all covered up. (We never knew if they even had hair). It was odd to hear them laugh, because in real life we never heard them laugh or even saw them smile. To sneak a peek at them, splashing in the warm water while playing games with a big ball was an unbelievable sight.

I stared in delighted amazement as I watched them actually playing with each other, jumping up and down and giggling with mildly subdued abandon. There was always fear in all of us to think we just might get caught. But for 'me', the exciting adventure was worth the risk of more daily punitive action.

One Tuesday afternoon, 'the me' was skipping obliviously around in this magical land, while loudly singing a nursery rhyme. Some older kids sadistically trapped 'me' in the narrow corner of a high metal fence and began pushing and calling out terrible names and laughing hideously: "You dirty Greek, you dirty Greek."

"I'm glad I'm a dirty Greek, I'm glad I'm a dirty Greek, so there. And what are you anyhow? Maybe you're a dirty Italian. Go away, you're mean and I hate all of you." Escaping from them, I ran to the top of the only slide, but they laughingly followed and continued to taunt 'me' with cruel words: "What is Leonides anyway? Is it a disease? Bet you can't jump from up there. Go ahead you dirty Greek, we dare you, we dare you."

"I'll show you, all of you." After jumping and falling unconscious to the ground, the "good" sister poured shivering cold water on my bruised and hurt body. She then cruelly shoved 'me', whimpering, to my little cot for the remainder of that warm summer afternoon; an afternoon that was meant for small children to play and be happy in.

I have tried so often to remember if Ethel and 'the me' ever played together in such a special paradise. No memory of this jumps out of my head.

The petite Sister Florence assigned every child a daily chore to do in the early morning hours after mass and before playtime. "Margaret, your particular task will be to keep our sacred grotto, clean and raked up."

Even though my stature was small, she handed what seemed to 'me' a very tall rake that was twice my height. In starting to clumsily rake up the leaves on that first morning of my designated assignment, a snake came slithering down the beautiful statue of the Virgin Mary. I was horrified- an emotion felt only once before, during the unforgettable flood. "This for sure is the devil." This was plausible because we had so often been told terrible stories about the devil.

With my whole body quivering in fright, I lifted the rake high over my head. When the snake slipped to the ground, I smashed it over and over until it didn't move anymore. A stream of nonstop hot tears rolled down my scared face, stinging and temporarily blinding 'me'.

I never knew what eventually happened to the "devil snake's" crushed body. Each day, ever so cautiously, I would creep into the sacred grotto, carefully looking for another "devil snake" with my rake at the ready. I never ever told anyone. I was afraid that killing a snake was worth being punished for, even if it was 'the devil', because we had been taught: 'Thou shalt not kill."

After two days of diligently raking up all the dried leaves, they were now neatly spread out to be burned for a much-anticipated marshmallow roast. "If our divine teacher Jesus could walk on anything, then maybe I can too, because Sister Theresa said: 'Margaret you are a good girl."

Thus taking my first confident step onto the burning coals with complete fearlessness, I severely burned my foot. I still have the scar. Sister Mary Matthew, with no sympathy, said, "Margaret, you are a very stupid child, stupid, stupid."

She roughly put salve on my foot. That hurt more than the burn, and her words hurt more than the salve: "Margaret, you can just sit on that log over there with your back to us. We don't want to look at such a stupid person."

Everyone, with lots of loud laughter, while in my crying tears I listened, as they had a marshmallow roast; even the nuns joined in the fun. "Where was Sister Theresa? Maybe she didn't need to come to this special summer camp. This could have been my first such roast if it weren't for my daily tormentor." Gentle Sister Florence kindly said, "Margaret you did such an exceptional job keeping the grotto tidy, and I'm sorry you burned your foot. We will be home next month, and your daily work, will be to carefully dust everything in our revered and blessed place of worship, our chapel. "

"But nope, I never dusted the statue of the Virgin Mary. I could not even look at her beautiful painted face, and I could never, never forget the devil snake."

SCENE NINE

Just like when he had stormed into and erupting thru the doors of the Detroit Protestant Asylum some years before, Papa arrived one day, unannounced, and came all but crashing through the heavy front doors. He was near to frenzied, with no respectful regard for anyone, as he loudly screamed at the Mother Superior: "They will come with me now!" To us, he yelled, "No, neither of you can take anything, not your doll, not anything. I don't care if you love it."

"Papa let 'me' get my little box of treasures, and my special pin, have to, have to, please, oh please let 'me'." I pulled away from him to get my secret box, all the while bitterly howling: "Please let 'me' say goodbye to Sister Theresa. Please, please. Stop hitting us, why are you mad? What bad things have we done?"

"Stop crying. No, you can't. We're leaving now, the bus is starting up and it won't wait for us."

With no control, he shoved us out the big beautiful carved doors and kicked us into the familiar roar of a blue and white roaring monster.

I never saw my first and only dear kind friend again. Sister Theresa was the one person to look at the 'me' with affection for many years to come. When she looked at 'me,' it was with care and even love. I felt worthwhile, almost exceptional. If 'the me' had known how to write then, I would have always sent her letters.

In being forced to leave my gentle Sister, hysterical and salty water fell out of my burning eyes that would not stop for days and nights. Papa was forever infuriated and enraged. He was without sympathy or understanding for my plight, and did not hold back a single one of his many intense slaps. "Stop that crying, stop it. What's wrong with you? Go to bed. Get out of my sight. I'll send you back to the home or somewhere else, get out."

I tried with great difficulty then, and even now, to visualize Sister Theresa's face through my warm tears, and how soft, kind and lovely she must have been. She often smiled at 'me'. My kind friend was the first in my life to ever touch 'me' with love. It truly changed my life forever.

"Ethel, don't you want to talk? I'm scared about what is going to happen to us, just like you, don't cry. We have to stick together. Let's talk." Again we were reluctantly carted out of St. Vincent's. We sat close together on the noisy bus, quietly whispering: "Papa is a nasty man. He doesn't know us and we don't know him, don't even want to know him. He makes 'me' squirm. Can he really be our Papa? Do you think he is ten feet tall? I'll never like him, he is just like mean Sister Mary Matthew and he always smells. Have you ever noticed the yellow stains on his fingers? I wonder what that means. Do you think it is a disease? Do you think maybe he is going to die?"

In spite of the frightful emotions that constantly lorded over 'me' when it came to this ogre of a man, my defiance (which was hidden most of the time) would turn out to be my permanent defense toward this unusually terrifying stranger.

Some type of generous godly courage, coming from somewhere, was in my very being. It helped 'me' during the few on and off years of barely knowing him and of being subjected to his insane whims. My life then had no rhyme or reason, and maybe there was none to be had in the life of John Leonides either. It seems odd to say or write his name.

That same strong courage held 'the me' tight during the brutal Sister Mary Matthew's unforgiving and never-ending ferocious harangues.

Though it would have been trouble-free to become a self-pitying victim, by some gift, I never did. 'The me' just knew "that" 'sister's problems were hers alone. "Where did this unusual and mature insight come from? I don't know, but it was there, and to a large extent it saved 'me'."

We had to board another oh-so-unsightly bus. It seemed that there was always a bus or some other means of transportation, impatiently waiting to take us with no care, to another mysterious and maybe frightful place. Papa suddenly blurted out: "You are going to New Jersey where you will live for now with your Aunt Mary, my sister. Call her Thea. That is the Greek name for aunt. Your mother is not dead. I told you that because I didn't know what else to tell you. She lives very near your Thea and maybe you will meet her. I have nothing more to say."

Then he stared out the window of the rapidly moving thunderous monster and almost immediately began to sleep and snore intermittently for the long hours of travelling many miles. In our bewilderment that followed hearing his terse and unexpected confession, we were left to conjure up the upsetting images of such a woman. In all truth, we were much too young for this overwhelming emotional task.

"Are you leaving us again Papa? Are you giving us away again? Don't you really want us? Will you say goodbye?"

My dear aunt Mary and Uncle George (a very crabby man) owned a sort of cute, old-time restaurant on Third Street in Elizabeth Port, New Jersey. The only way to keep warm in the bitter

New Jersey winters was by the black coal burning big potbelly stove: "It was quaint and I loved it."

Once a week, one of my jobs was to carry a twenty-five pound bag of coal to their little restaurant from a lumber company down the block. It was very heavy for someone weighing less than fifty pounds, so most times it was easier to drag it. Occasionally people would laugh, but more often than not a man, here or there, would come to my much-needed rescue.

We were enrolled in a nearby Catholic school (always Catholic, hmmm), and were unquestionably expected to work in Thea's cozy restaurant after school. "And we wanted to, as it was far better than St. Vincent's and the wretched Sister. But I could not help missing Sister Theresa and her private talks with 'me'."

Because of Ethel's full-blown maturity, the boys were always tagging after her, calling out stuff not understood by 'me'. But Ethel knew it all and found it much fun to tease and torment the eager young boys just entering puberty or beyond.

Aunt Mary became increasingly frantic, not knowing how to care for or understand her mature niece. Thea was unforgivably overworked, forever tired, and unhappy. She never laughed, even when someone was trying to coax a smile out of her. She was about forty-five, but she looked much older and more tired than that, and so did Uncle George.

By some means or other she got in touch with my unfeeling father, her brother: "I cannot take care of Ethel any longer. The boys are all after her. You have to come for her now, but please let Margie to stay with me."

Ethel was callously delivered, on a very cold day, to live with Sophie. "How did she get there, why and when?" Sophie would turn out to be more violent to her than Sister Mary Matthew had ever been. It was destined to be a calamity of a nightmare for my poor discarded sister. Another abandonment, another time in her life to feel deserted, unloved and not wanted by anyone. Another time to try finding love, or what she called love, anywhere she could.

A little digression again please.

When at St. Vincent's, my curiosity often strayed to older children who hardly ever got scolded or punished. They forever and a day sat very upright and smiled a lot. Somehow they knew the "secret." "I'll do that and maybe punishments won't be heaped on 'me' so often, and maybe I will be liked. I'll tell Ethel so she can do the same thing." But no, she was too alone and forsaken.

Ethel's enticing and forever evil companions were fear, envy, irate jealousy and a fervent self-pity: "I have never been happy a day in my life, even though I've been married a couple of miserable times, have held down two jobs, have my own home and brought two sons into the world." Those were her self-indulgent words to 'me' not long before she left this abhorrent world, as she regretfully saw it.

In her mid seventies, she suffered a fatal stroke, collapsing on her little kitchen floor, a kitchen she had decorated in meticulous good taste. In many ways, Ethel had developed a keen sense of expensive style.

Her eldest son died years ago from an incurable disease. My sister's remains were cremated according to her wishes and handled by her youngest boy. They had a very unhappy and cantankerous relationship. There was no service for either of them, it was as if they never were. A heart breaker.

She was all by her lonesome self and still unloved. It was unmistakable that no one could ever fill the emptiness that enveloped her, share happiness with her, or provide her some degree of contentment and peace.

As it would miserably turn out, not a living soul could eradicate the heart rendering memories of her poignant years of neglect, abuse, abandonment, punishment and the total invalidation. Her incredibly dark memories refused to heal and with no consciousness, she was emotionally not strong enough to acknowledge and reconcile them. "Did I love my sister and feel tender compassion and sorrow for her always? Did I wish and long for a close relationship with her? Did I want us to share our lives? Did everyone enjoy her sense of humor when she was able to muster it up? Do I weep for her even today, and all the yesterdays? Yes to all of this and of course."

So often my daily and silent prayer was that she could have enjoyed some bit of contentment, if not happiness. It eventually appeared even the slightest possibility of a tranquil life was cast out early by the disconsolate and evil shadows that she was unable to recognize or crack through. "What could anyone do to exterminate the dissolution she so despondently drowned in, to perhaps help her mend and feel whole?"

Such sweetness was never to lovingly embrace or liberate her. It would be easy and accurate to say that her handsome boys or her several husbands had no inkling of the torments Ethel was unable to recognize even in her honest attempts.

Because of Ethel's pernicious denial, the people in her life could not begin to appreciate the treacherous sorrows that resulted in her persistently truly wicked and entangled behavior. Her negative persona undoubtedly became her protective armor, but because of it, no one could afford to take the rancid likelihood of coming to her needed aid.

She often treated others in the equivalent hurtful and hateful manners she had been dealt with. Did she understand this about herself, that "hurt people, hurt people?"

"What miraculous gift was generously wrapped around 'the me' with a pretty pink ribbon, early on? How did I escape from that extraordinary convoluted tornado of hers? We were of the same heritage, with the same frightful dragging up. This bizarre difference in our personalities remains a perplexing riddle." My heart fills with sweet gratitude every day for my life-saving gift. At the same time, I cannot help but undergo great sadness and compassion for the human being that would forever be my disturbed and cheerless sibling.

It occurs to me quite momentarily that someone wrote or said: "Evil is as evil does." Does this reflective philosophy apply to the once naïve and beseeching soul that was simply seeking her share of deserved love and approval?

Surely that could not be too much to ask out of life? Did she ask the question of herself, as we all do? "What am I existing for and why am I here?" Oscar Wilde profoundly, but in somewhat of a jaded mood wrote, "We are all in the gutter, but some of us are looking at the stars."

If there is such a thing as 'another life', a 'here-after', perhaps Ethel will opt for one, in her next time around, that will generously bestow upon her all that was blatantly and viciously stolen in this harsh life of hers.

A SKINNY ORPHAN GIRL

Lyrics by Margie Belrose
Dedicated, with no compunctions, to myself

A SKINNY ORPHAN GIRL WITH LITTLE HAIR,

AND JUST ONE TINY CURL

THEY ALL THOUGHT IT BEST SO THEY COULD REST

AND NOT BE BOTHERED WITH THE SKINNY ORPHAN GIRL

I LONGED FOR TREASURES TO CALL MY OWN

MAYBE A DOLL TO LOVE

I COULD NOT EVEN IMAGINE A HOME

BUT THEN I GREW UP AND GATHERED PRECIOUS THINGS

THAT MEANT SOMETHING, NOT JUST SAD DREAMS

THEY FILLED MY LIFE WITH JOY

I EVEN KNEW GIRLS AND SOME BOYS

SOMEHOW I HAD A FEW TOYS

I MADE SOME FRIENDS, AND UNTIL MY VERY END

I KNOW I AM NO LONGER A SKINNY ORPHAN GIRL

I'VE HAD A DOLL, A HOME, SOME PRECIOUS THINGS

I HAVE TREASURES AND MOST OF ALL

I HAVE AND KNOW LOVE (a plus)

© 2009 Margie Belrose

SCENE TEN

"Thea, thank you for letting me live with you for now. I'm happy today. You're kind and your big hugs make 'me' feel good. I love you my Aunt Mary."

As 'the me' was barely a ten-year-old working in their restaurant most nights until twelve or one in the morning, being late for school, or not at all, became my chronic and helpless habit. Many mornings I just could not wake up, and a truant officer would come banging loudly on Thea's front door. Then I would silently squirrel my way into a dark closet and drift off to welcome sleep again.

St. Michaels sent my Thea several threatening letters to no avail, and life continued in the same confusing manner. At times I was so sleepy and tired I could not make it to the comfort of my bed. Without realizing it, 'the me' would crawl into the cold porcelain bathtub to then mercifully drift into temporary undisturbed slumber. Uncle George would find 'me' there on his early morning trips to the bathroom: "What is wrong with you, are you crazy? Get the hell out of there and go to school." (As said, "a crabby man"). If and when I was finally able to trudge my troubled body the short distance to St. Michaels, I would secretly creep into the cloakroom and wrap my worn-out coat around my sleepy body. There would always be the other children's coats to nestle into and then gentle, grateful slumber would over take 'me'. "Sister, I can't wake up, so tired."

"Try to wake up, Margie, don't cry, you won't get into trouble, I promise."

"Being called Margie by now was better than the way Sister Mary Matthew hatefully screeched "Margaret." Her stern voice always sent shivers throughout my body." The same was true for joyless Ethel, who detested her first name because of the mean tone of voice 'that sister' would use. Eventually she changed her first name five times trying to drown out that menacing voice.

I loved cleaning my dear aunt's home. To 'me', it was a warm place that spelled safety every day; at least for the short time my father permitted 'me' to live there.

On Fridays after school, when tiredness did not take over me, it was fun planting wonderful smelling mint that I would savor close to my nose. It grew all over her little garden, and I, not knowing then that mint could grow anywhere, thought of myself as quite the gardener.

I can still remember the way the water would make her cellar smell when washing down the brick walls. One Friday while standing in a puddle of that same warm water I reached for the light switch and was crashed to the basement wall, nearly electrocuting myself. This was my fourth encounter with another possible death: "Oh dear. Will this threat to a life I've just begun to live never end?"

Thea's daughter Tess, owned a rather large and successful dance studio on Broad Street in Elizabeth. Knowing my future was to be a dancer, I asked, "Please Thea, let me take classes at Tess's studio."

"Margie, yes, dear one, yes that is your dream to dance. You can take the bus up Jersey Street by yourself, every Saturday morning. Can you wake up in time to go? Be sure to pay attention during your lesson, and then she will expect you to clean her studio as payment.

Afterwards you can walk the four blocks to the Liberty Vaudeville Theatre.

Here is fifty cents. I know directions confuse you, so remember to turn left by the drug store to catch the bus back when you leave the theatre. Let me tie this ribbon on your left wrist to remind you."

"Thea, will you tie the pink ribbon on my wrist?"

Oh, Saturdays were my happy days that made up for so many unhappy ones.

Most Sundays my dear Thea prepared a big pot of rigatoni with a special Greek sauce for her 'regular' customers. I will never forget that mouth-watering taste and smell.

When the suffocating and muggy summer Sundays arrived. 'the me' was given permission to go to the nearly Olympic size swimming pool at the end of the port.

The blue-green water mischievously urged 'me' to float there all day until my body turned red and wrinkly, even though I still did not know how to swim. One Sunday a disgusting boy tried to grab 'the me' between my legs, under the water. A loud cry for help forced him to quickly paddle away.

I'm a Leo, a fire sign, but with my love of the water, the beach, my morning shower, and my tub, I feel I should have been a water sign. Most Leos are also destined to be in the theatre. Therefore being in it is where I have to be, want to be, need to be, passionately love to be, and will always be.

Very late at night, it was quite common to hear Tess having hateful screaming tirades with her parents. These were the same doting parents who loved her very much and sacrificed heavily to buy her a studio. She spit out dreadful words at them, using the "F"

word, long before that word was common the way it is in today's often-unkind world.

Thea's daughter had fallen in love with a man of the Jewish religion and was going to marry him against her parents' fierce and pleading wishes. Aunt Mary's family all derived from a long and revered line of Greek Orthodox people, priests and monks.

For Tess to marry a man of the Jewish faith was beyond what they could accept and they didn't, just couldn't. Nevertheless, Tess did marry Merv, causing her parents to be deeply hurt and saddened.

He owned a small corner cigar shop a few blocks from her dance studio. It was rumored that his store was the front for a numbers gambling racket. Eventually Merv's illegal numbers game was investigated. He was arrested and brought from New Jersey to California- (why California? Don't know)- to spend several years in a cushy California jail. "Guess the rumors were true."

Of course, Tess followed him to California, and ironically moved not far from my own theatre. This was a fact not known to 'me' for several years; it was more than a weird state of affairs. It's so strange and bizarre that there is really no room or reason to write about this implausible situation in this book of mine.

But long before such drastic and major changes in their lives, she gave up her studio and in its place gave birth to two daughters. Sometime before Merv's arrest they quickly moved to another city in New Jersey. Before all these unsettling happenings in their lives, that had nothing to do with my life, my dear Thea slumped to the sidewalk from a fatal heart attack. This unhappy and unexpected event was very near her home that was loved and happily cleaned by 'me', and where safety generously looked down on 'me' during the tenth year of my very childlike and daunting life.

I don't know if my generous hearted Thea ever reconciled with her inconsiderate and selfish daughter. The story of Tess is a whole different and cruel matter. Not good in any way. Not for this book, as I've said, and more than likely, not for any.

When my sweet Thea unexpectedly left this world, and I was no longer living with her for some years, the story goes:

"Tess and her now-deceased brother, (who at one time, when I was very young, attempted to rape 'me'), were impatient to descend upon their charitable mother's home, belongings, money, and a rather liberal estate. They greedily scavenged, like killing dogs, through every conceivable profitable belonging, even to the point of stealing from one another."

During my unforgettable and safe year in my Thea's home on Magnolia Avenue, there were many obviously immoral things by her two adult children happening in their household. It was easy to see that Tess and her brother were crammed with many devious, selfish and dishonest qualities.

Even though my years then were still quite young, I realized they were not good people. I will forever believe there is no saving grace for either of them. I am ashamed of them, as they should be of themselves and cannot help but deny them as my relatives.

SCENE ELEVEN

It turned out that I had a half-sister (gosh that seems strange to say) who I never knew named Frances. I did not know such a person existed until she phoned from Sophie's house one Saturday, inviting 'me' to their home to visit Ethel. I don't remember Frances being there- Sophie had her call to invite 'me' because, I can only determine, she was a coward.

I hadn't seen my older sister in many months, and when she appeared at the door that Sunday afternoon, she looked so much like a mature woman that it was startling.

I was in Sophie's well-organized kitchen making small talk while trying to get acquainted with her, all the while tapping my feet to some radio music. I was, after all, learning to dance. Sophie yelled- really yelled — "Stop that noise!"

But the child in 'me' impulsively needed to keep tapping anyway, and without warning, she gave 'me' a hard smack on the head. She kept beating me, screaming and chasing me around the house. Ethel simply stood aside in her own terror-stricken demeanor, unable to come forward and protect 'me'.

Keep in mind, dear patient reader; this was the first time I had ever met Sophie. I raced for my coat, attempting to exit through the front door, which I knew would be the only escape from her flailing, angry arms and screeching voice. From this one experience from hell, I can only assume the magnitude of unbearable physical and verbal abuses Ethel must have suffered at the wicked hands of Sophie, for very little reason.

Some months later, on a Friday after school, while loudly singing my heart out and washing thirty three cottage type windows in the sun porch of Thea's home, my sister appeared a short distance down the street, carrying two huge bags of 'things'. She was almost stumbling alongside a slow-moving taxi. Sophie was comfortably riding in the cab, and upon exiting the taxi; she viciously gave Ethel a mean kick at the same time reaching for the front door. My sister fell, and just as if she was still two years old, Sophie hit her in the head while screaming: "Pick everything up and hurry, you nothing thing." This is so heart breaking, it is almost impossible to write or think about.

When the front door flew open, this callous so-called mother shoved Ethel in, with another equally mean push, screaming, "Here, take her, she's your sister! I don't want her. She's a nothing." In my defiance toward this crazed woman who was easy to detest, I yelled, "You didn't want us when we were babies and you don't want us now. I hate you, I hate you, I hate you, you've never been a mother, instead you, not Ethel, are a nothing thing and a mean coward!"

My sister stood transfixed and unable to do anything, except cringe and actually turn her back on the horrendous scene. Sophie could not wait to deliver one powerful blow after another with her purse, cornering 'me' on the steps to the upstairs as she persisted in her wild attack with unleashed hatred. She was unbelievably ugly in her rage. The handle of her purse broke. At this point I did not know whether to laugh or cry, so I did both simultaneously. "You didn't want us ever and now we don't want you. Get out of my Thea's house."

This was the second time in my life that I ever saw this disturbed, barely a human thing.

Again Ethel was abandoned. Yes, I too, had been punished, abandoned, invalidated and deserted, but my blessing was that two people LOVED 'the me': kind Sister Theresa, the first one to care in her nun way, and now my dear Thea.

Ethel did not seem to be loved and obviously was incapable of knowing how to return love when it would try to entice her into its' folds: "How could she? She never acknowledged love on any level when it attempted to beguile her. She never felt it. Sadly, she didn't even know how it could feel."

To receive and give love is surely a plus, and happiness is the reward. To be deprived of and reject love most certainly is a minus and there is no reward.

SCENE TWELVE

Papa, in his usual hateful way, arrived to fetch Ethel—his unwanted, distraught and disoriented daughter. With instinctive fear and distrust, I snuck into a closet and hid among the clothes, so he never saw 'me'. I do not know when or how they left or what had transpired.

Aunt Mary later said they moved to Utica, New York. That was the start of the person called my father and my unhappy sister actually living together off and on over the years.

Papa knew her somewhat, but never knew 'me'. I'm thankful. This Margie person was blessedly the FORTUNATE daughter. Many months after papa came for Ethel, he called from Utica: "Margie, I am coming for you tomorrow. Get your things ready, I will have no time to wait."

I began to shake with the all too familiar terror always felt when hearing his voice or when around him. Even thinking about him unsettled 'me' through and through. "Thea, I'm not going to pack, then Papa can't take 'me', can he? Help 'me'!"

Papa appeared at his sisters' home, as he had threatened, with his customary curt and frightening hot temper surrounding him. "Get your things, we are leaving now."

"How can we papa? There is no bus waiting." In desperation, while crying I begged, "Please let 'me' stay, Papa, I am happy here. I love Thea." Her son, Johnny, was on a short leave from the Navy:

"Help 'me,' Johnny, help, don't let Papa take 'me'." He did not or could not help. My father hatefully pushed his sister, my own dear aunt, down on the floor. She was not a little person, but a short, pudgy, and sweet lady. Papa vehemently shoved Johnny aside in his customary aggressive manner.

This cruel father, with pure detestable vengeance, started for 'me', but I pulled away from his menacing grasp and scrambled up to the attic to the abode that my young self had fixed up. "I have to get my little box of treasures."

Papa, taking two steps at a time, literally dragged 'me' down the flight of stairs by my scraggly hair. He was still screeching and continuing to curse and push. I tripped at the bottom of the steps; he jerked 'me' up with a hurtful kick.

He didn't care. In my eyes, he was barely a human being, with no compassion, kindness or goodness.

"Who was the worse, which inconceivable creature was embodied with terminal evil? Sister Mary Matthew, Sophie, or my father? They all three must have come out of the same infected cocoon." Their cruel sins engulfed my sister and I during so much of our early lives. "How was it possible that three separate evil individuals could wreak so much devastation and havoc on us?" They always ruthlessly left crushed human rubble in their wake- a path of wreckage that would take years to live through and had no sweet way of truly healing completely.

I sensed, by some measure of intelligence at a very early age, that these bedeviled people came into my life with their own neurotic baggage of unholy stuff that had nothing, absolutely nothing, to do with 'me'.

Somehow, this person, called 'me' was able to disassociate myself, logically (not emotionally) and in large measure from their cruel insanity and sickness. I unconsciously knew to step away and look at them, albeit squeamishly, as threatening vile strangers, while desperately seeking to find an escape route somehow.

Of course this instinct could not be articulated at such a young age, but that god-given knowledge was steadily there, then as now. By some golden gift, this Margie person was never as severely scarred or victimized as my older sister. Ethel's abuse was grossly inflicted on a daily basis, from three despicable human beings: Sister Mary Matthew, Papa, or Sophie.

"Did Papa ever talk to his sister, my Thea, again? Don't know." During that inconceivable incident at my Thea's home, Ethel appeared down the street to be distant and withdrawn. No greetings were exchanged, but as always, she looked incredibly broken down. She admitted at times that she was without self-esteem or joy for the whole of her forlorn life. Ethel did make a concerted effort to be 'normal', but she was inadvertently incapable of escaping her agonized past or turning away from her depressing fears, terrors and loneliness.

Surely those tumultuous emotions could not help but crowd into her troubled psyche every day of her tangled life. Thus, alleviating any possibility of happiness and security, leading to an inhuman and tortured life that would end in her mid-seventies.

"These things can only be expressed and actually written down, as an adult. I acknowledge all of this now that I've lived my own life's experiences of sorrow, betrayals, abandonment, punishments, love, hurt, hate, disappointments, fear, death and childbirth.

I did not appreciate these indistinct observations in my early years, and they are being uttered only now in retrospect. There is in 'me' a deep respect and understanding for what we all (you, the reader of this book, and 'me' the writer) have surely experienced to varying degrees in our exclusive existence. Every individual without exception, has lived their own unique story that belongs to them alone that deserves to possibly be shared, if not already."

We were on yet another oh-so-familiar mode of transportation, which had been parked around the corner from my Thea's house and where Ethel had been waiting.

With a mighty growl and a cough of smoky exhaust from the giant vehicle, Ethel with hesitation came forward and we were sped off to a new destination called Johnstown, New York.

We both knew we were about to face the same inexcusable and uncertain times that occurred whenever this extraordinarily evil person named Papa appeared.

He would, with malice and with no conscious thought, surround himself in a heavy black cloud of hatred and misery. His toxic cloud would absolutely overtake our milieu, nearly choking us with permeating abhorrence.

We sat huddled together, afraid to even talk. In our tremulous silence we hoped Papa would not lash out for any of his senseless reasons- something he might well have done with no control, even on the crowded public bus.

We arrived in Johnstown, not knowing the plans of our cagey monstrosity of a man. In the small apartment Papa had secured, there stood in the kitchen a charming, wrought-iron cooking stove from a long ago past. Papa prepared a wonderful smelling stew on the stove and went out early to roam around, leaving it to simmer. As we slept, the coal stove was burning and deadly fumes began to fill the small apartment.

Papa came back to find firemen had already been called. While they were busy trying to clear the fumes out, Papa was blowing in my face with his fowl breath, trying to waken 'me'. Not knowing what was happening, I slowly came to and promptly slapped him in the face- a reflex, but a good one. "Was that moment of payback a good thing? Yes, I think so."

This was now my fifth escape from death, but who can possibly be counting? We never entered school during what must have been a short stay in Johnstown. Soon the all-too-familiar, fanatical scene erupted: "Get your things we must leave right now!"

"Ethel, does everyone live and talk like this man we call our papa? Something is wrong, I just know it is, don't you think so too? Let's try to run away from him forever, 'cause he will always be the same mean and crazy person. We have to try and find a way to break away from him and his madness."

"Margie, where would we go? We're just kids, and we have no money. I wish we could too. We'll try to make plans anyway."

SCENE THIRTEEN

Once again on a very long, long ride, the only words uttered by such a bastard, right before his loud snoring, were:

"We are moving to Huntington, West Virginia, where you will enroll in a school." Papa rented a second floor apartment next door to the third person in my life that would unselfishly lavish 'me' with affection. Tall and slender Dorcus Holt and my father became instant business partners opening the Eagle Café. Curiously enough, in a few months we happily moved in with her.

One Saturday afternoon while waitressing in their restaurant, Ethel had a life-threatening appendicitis attack. Papa began yelling and pushing 'me' around, and finally he smacked 'ME'. One of the customers jumped out of a booth in complete disgust: "What is wrong with you, are you nuts? Your other daughter is the one that is very sick; she can't even stand up. Get out of my way you crazy man, I'll take her to the hospital in my car." Ethel had her ruptured appendix removed just in time. How she got back from the hospital I don't know, and I never visited her. Did Papa?

Her unexpected operation would also manifest itself as a continuing disruptive memory. It became another dramatic occurrence she found difficult to let go of. To this day the whole incident seems bizarre, as so many others.

Too many to write about, or think about, that I have so often tried to forget.

Late one night, in passing Dorcus' open bedroom door, I saw that she and my father were sleeping together. Blinking my sleepy eyes, while staring for untold minutes in disbelief, I attempted to silently catch my gasping breath. "Did he kiss her? Did he hold her? Did he say 'I love you'? Did he talk to her?" I wondered what that would all be like. These were things 'the me' had no comprehension of, from him, ever.

It was on another late night when I overheard Dorcus whispering: "I would like to adopt Margie. I can do so much for her and I love her. But I can only adopt one of your girls." Papa became unreasonably angry and refused. Ethel heard the conversation and justifiably became very hurt and resentful.

Dorcus was the only person to that point in my life to actually say, "I love Margie." No, must take that back, because I just recalled my Thea would lovingly whisper to 'the me' many times, with tender kisses, "Little Margie, I love you and you are a sweet dear child." She would gather 'the me' to her generous bosom, as tears of happiness would trickle down my eager, grateful face.

Another night, soon after hearing that disturbing conversation, Papa was frenziedly screaming at Dorcus. I don't know why. The next day he walked to the Eagle Café, locked the door, and never went back.

I have often wondered if such irresponsibility was one of the reasons he unpredictably left various cities so quickly, in a fury, and never with an explanation.

Later in our stroll, I know I will be compelled to ask this disheartening question again, that seemingly has no answer.

"Did he have to run away owing gullible and trusting people money?"

Oh, God, we were now on another oh-so-familiar means of transportation, traveling very rapidly to a place far away: Ely, Nevada. There were no good-byes to Dorcus. I never heard from her. 'The me' would forever miss her. Dorcus was a kind lady who said, "I love Margie." Grateful 'me' had generously wrapped bushels of love and countless hugs around her during every day of our short life together. I didn't know how to write her.

In Ely, my father was invited to be the priest of a lovely new Greek Orthodox Church. With our arms crossed over our chests the way Papa insisted we do, we quietly sat there for his first and only Sunday mass.

Everything looked perfect in our inexperienced eyes, something we had never seen or been part of before. We did not know our priest/father like this, in a beautiful robe and with everyone showing him unfamiliar respect. Then again, we had never seen him in much of our lives anyway or in anything at all, so this was incredibly new, weird and spectacular.

At the conclusion of the long service, (which was even longer than the Catholic masses), a Greek lady invited our family of three to her home for dinner and a party, along with others, as was the church custom. Lots of delicious-smelling Greek food we had never seen or tasted before was arranged on a long dining room table. As several men arrived, they began to play exciting music on unusual instruments that were shiny and gorgeous.

I was still just a kid, but this was a completely overwhelming celebration that I respected beyond words. It was magical-for a few hours. Papa began to gulp down untold glasses of Greek wine. The evening was strange—such a special party, and our first one ever. Sadly it would be our last.

My eyes opened wide to see him as the incredible lead in a Greek dance we had never seen. It was amazing and we were astonishingly proud. But the more wine he guzzled, the meaner and distraught he became, his hot temper was on the verge of exploding. Biting, offensive words, following no provocation, soon came out of his vulgar mouth. It was "F" this and "F" that. In retrospect, I realize he could not prevent or save himself from self-destructing, which he had undoubtedly been doing all his disturbed life.

Of course, this was the lovely beginning and the terrifying end of his being the priest of such a beautiful church. It was perched on a grassy green hill, near the edge of town, and held the possibility of a "conventional" life for the three of us.

It would have been nice to live such a life with my Papa, to know him, respect him, maybe to find mutual love between us. We never had even a simple conversation; consequently I truly did not know him, ever. There is no memory of a touch by him in any fatherly way- there was only the never-ending hitting, hitting, hitting. What relentlessly rings in my ears, to this very day of my adult life that is now entering its' twilight years, is his screaming, swearing. At times, I can still feel him pushing and smacking 'the me' in a phantom like way.

We left, hardly able to believe that our Papa could behave so badly. We walked back to the house he had rented. It was a tiny house that stood next to a small but incredibly putrid garbage heap. Papa began to stumble—a symptom we now recognized as signifying drunkenness. All of a sudden he stopped, and pointed to a rather tall building: "Margie, if I told you to jump from the top of that building and into my arms, would you?" "Yes, Papa."

"No, no, I would take my arms away. Never trust anyone, not

even your Papa." Then for an inexplicable reason, he probably didn't grasp himself, he became exceedingly agitated and violent. With a brutal vengeance, he came at 'me' with his eyes seething hatred. Terrified of him, and cowardly hiding behind my bigger sister, he began to ferociously hit her over and over with no restraint. "Who was he really attacking? Was Sophie blocking his reasonable ability to recognize his despicable and misplaced behavior?"

Shame filled 'me', and still does, even today, for letting Ethel succumb to the outrageous and unforeseen beating intended for Margie. "Did he teach us to never trust? For my sister, I don't really know, but for 'me', NO, in fact, by some peculiar rational the exact opposite is the truth."

After that unforgettable night out of hell, my father, with no shame or personal pride, opened a small hamburger/hot dog "joint" on the main street of Ely.

We had to scurry after school to work there, at which point he would immediately and compulsively leave, going out to gamble in what we knew as a sleazy bar down the street. He would then recklessly indulge in his usual drunken addiction. After all, this was Nevada, and drinking and gambling was what he lived for. "I believe this was the first time that we actually came to realize papa was a true, die-hard alcoholic."

We were expected to manage the odd-shaped restaurant. I don't know how we did it: the grill, the hamburgers, the hot dogs, the supplies, cleaning, all the other stuff, the people, the money and the cash register. "Good grief, we were just this side of being adolescents."

For some mysterious reason- our grade cards appeared to have typos or were just unreadable. They suggested that both Ethel and I were in the eighth instead of the seventh grade. It was the second time I had been moved up a year, this time with no credit to myself. Ethel unreasonably resented me for it. She ended up being forced to repeat her eighth year because her grades were so pathetically low. Meanwhile, I graduated into high school with my own pathetic, but passable grades.

We had become good friends with the Bartsas family, who bought the budding 'me' a special brown and beige graduation dress. They came to my eight-grade ceremony, and then we celebrated with a special dinner in their beautiful home.

My father and sister did not share my experience on that exceptional evening, which became a right of passage of my blossoming life. It was easy to stay in touch with the dear Bartsas family for many years. Unfortunately, when they moved from Ely, we lost touch.

Right after my own uneven eight-grade was completed, Papa sold, (or might have just walked out of), the curiously narrow restaurant. "We are moving to Sacramento, California. Get your things. We are leaving now, there is no time to lose."

"We should have been used to the erratic actions of our "not nice father." Did serious trouble continually stalk him everywhere?" At times the thought stumbled thru my mind that maybe the police would somehow come to arrest us for something papa had done illegally. That seemed to be the only logical explanation for our abrupt departures.

We stepped into anther smelly vehicle and headed for the predictably long ride to Sacramento, California.

We had probably only lived in Ely about eight months. It was the second time I lived with such a mean and eruptive stranger. Possibly I lived with that man less than one and a half years (off and on) during my entire circuitous young life. However, Ethel lived with him as an adult now and then for longer periods of time.

I had just turned thirteen, and Ethel, was fourteen. The huffing and puffing bus pulled on its brakes and we set foot on California soil. It was eleven p.m. and still hot when we touched down on the small farm town of Lodi, California, in late August of 1943.

SCENE FOURTEEN

The thunderous grey and white bus, where we had uncomfortably sat or slept for hours, could not continue to Sacramento at that late hour. Sometimes my thoughts would wander to practical problems: "Where did we go to the bathroom or eat in all the fanatical and hurried bus traveling times of our lives? Oh I must confess: my young life never stops bewildering 'me'."

Papa put us up in a cheap hotel, "The Travelers", located on a street known as "skid row." We did not know it then but this was a corruptible street to even walk on, certainly for two unrefined teenage girls. We quickly crawled into a bed for much-needed rest while papa wondered out to drink. Coincidentally, he came upon several coffee houses on that creepy street where Greek men from his very own Greek village of Platanos spent time. They drank, played cards and talked of politics all through the night.

The days would find Papa snoozing away. Then at early evening, guided by some inner clock, he would wake up to scramble out for yet another night of despicable behavior with his cronies. Practically speaking again: "When did Ethel and I eat, and where, what did we do in the daytime?" So many mysteries that will never be solved. After several weird weeks, Papa made an unexpected announcement that we would not move to Sacramento, but would continue to live in Lodi. He bought a grimy restaurant, and told us, with all the 'kindness' he could rally up: "Go to school."

We didn't even know where any school was, and had to timidly ask directions from an annoyed and short-tempered hotel clerk.

We moved into a rooming house; one room for us, the other for Papa. Ethel took or stole my things, as was her persistent tendency, and on our first edgy night there she gave me a doozy of a nosebleed. This was not the first or the last time she'd physically hurt 'me', but I never fought with her. I could not have won. She was bigger, stronger and ruthless. "I didn't know how to physically fight then, and I don't know now. I don't want to know."

Papa opened his greasy-spoon restaurant on Sacramento Street, or "skid row." Ethel and I enrolled in two separate schools, three weeks late. Because of our tardy entrance, and our horrible experiences in the past, we were filled with a constant trepidation that overtook our growing bodies.

Ethel re-entered the eight grade and was humiliated. She held 'me' responsible for her having to repeat the year. She still did not do well and barely passed out of middle school. I would surmise she just wasn't a 'student'. Meanwhile, I was an intimidated freshman at Lodi High, and my days were filled with continuous apprehensions and nervous anxiety. 'The me' began to seriously bite 'my' nails to the quick.

Because of enrolling so late, the counselor signed 'me' up for "bonehead English." (What an embarrassing description). In spite of the intense hours of useless efforts and guidance, I could not catch up until my junior year. "I ask myself, where did the nerve to write come from? It is just that: nerve. Cause my English ain't so good." "Now, Charlie, this must be a joke, right?"

Even as a new freshman, 'the me' had the sublime naïveté to plop myself down on the top steps of the school's main building at lunchtime. The concrete steps, unknown to 'me' then, were for the exclusive rich 400. Even so, I gobbled down my peanut butter and jelly sandwich, followed by a gulp of milk, while sitting there, sunning myself during lunchtime. The overt looks that bombarded 'me' cried out: "Leave you don't belong here. Go away." However, I kept sitting up straight and smiling- the lesson I had learned, though not early enough, at St. Vincent's.

I just didn't scoot off, and soon the '400' were comfortable with my being there. Certain girls and a few boys even became my life long friends. After several months a few girls invited 'me'to join their club. I don't think 'me' did, or maybe I just couldn't. "But isn't that a trip, for someone like 'me', a castaway?"

SCENE FIFTEEN

Lodi High's required dress code for girls was dark skirts, sweaters, and no see-through blouses. "How fortunate for 'me', since I didn't have very many clothes. Where did the few I had even come from? I had no money to shop, and didn't even know how to go into a store and shop."

Two black pleated skirts were my 'uniform' for almost four years. I also managed to acquire a few second hand blouses and three angora sweaters, plus a pair of used brown and white saddle shoes that I cleaned to spotlessness ever night. I also scrounged up bobby socks to match my three sweaters; this was my every day fashion ensemble.

"Of course you can see, without a doubt, that this ninth grader was a trendsetter, a fashion plate." I took up sewing in my home economic class, so I was able to make a few things for my last two years of high school. To my teacher's surprise, I even sewed a beautiful grey tailored jacket. "Hmmm...wonder what ever happened to that magnificent creation of mine?"

I was so ashamed of my life, ashamed to have to walk to that dirty street and loathsome restaurant every day. Ashamed when Papa would appear every once in awhile, in front of the school lawn. I would turn, with all haste, in the opposite direction, pretending to not know the man who was all but falling over, slurring "Margie!" In thinking back, I know some school friends began to sense my shame and even looked after 'me'. Especially Ruthie, "That was kind and perceptive of you Ruthie, my forever friend, never to be forgotten."

Every day of that first year, I would walk quickly through the school halls with my head held up too high. The 'me' never looked in any direction while trembling from head to toe, just trying to get to my next class several halls away. Some people said: "She's just stuck up." But it was embarrassment and fear that consumed my scared, skinny body. Even to timidly walk up to sharpen my pencil, these knees of mine, with my St. Vincent's bumps on them, would visibly wobble while cold sweat poured out of 'me'. By the time my assigned desk welcomed this quivering person back I would almost cry out of shear relief. 'The me' did not realize that nervous sweat had a distinct unpleasant odor. I soon found out.

In spite of a less than happy and precarious beginning, 'the me' finished the first year with very little damage to 'my' vulnerable spirit. In fact, Ruthie invited 'me' to stay overnight several times during my high school years. It was always an amazing and exciting pleasure to be in a regular home with regular people. The experience would always turn out to be something that was completely new that allowed 'the me' to feel like "one of them" even though I wasn't.

We two sisters had to clamber as fast as possible after school every dismal day, be it rain or shine, to waitress in Papa's revolting restaurant. It was truly embarrassing to be in such a place. The harsh father of ours didn't need any provocation to slap us around, in front of customers or otherwise. He would lash out uncontrollably. One evening he gave Ethel a brutal black eye, with no feelings or concern for what he had viciously done. A customer advised 'me' to: "Put a piece of steak on her black eye. That will help it to heal."

And that is what I did for my injured sister. It was a gesture my father paid no attention to or cared about in the slightest. "Ethel, don't cower, stand up for yourself. We'll do it together. Don't be afraid. But she was unable to protect or help herself, she was trapped and could do nothing but grovel in his merciless presence.

Despite the fact that I had a very immature concept of life, even so it was obvious to 'me' that her full-out terror of him was beyond redemption. She forever longed for and desperately needed his love and approval. He did not have it in his very young soul to give of himself in any compassionate capacity; to his two abused and neglected daughters or anyone. "How could he? He didn't know us. He didn't love us. He didn't want us. He callously threw us away over and over. We were disposable. We were nothing to him, just a big fat zero. He had dreadful lifelong problems of his own making and remaking."

Papa viewed the two of us as major hindrances in his life.

One evening, customers were shocked when they witnessed Papa coming at 'me' with a large metal spoon. "Papa, don't you ever hit 'me' again. You will never see 'me' even one more time in this atrocious bed of ugliness you call a restaurant!"

"I am your Papa and you will work here and that is the only way you will eat!"

"I don't even like what you cook, so who cares if I ever eat again. You say you're a priest. You should be kind and good and instead you are forever angry and hateful. You're never nice. You hit, you drink, you swear, you smell. If you are a priest, what are you doing owning and working in this revolting restaurant? I'm leaving now forever. Come on Ethel, let's go together." But no, she could not. Incredibly, she just stood as if transfixed and could only quiver. I walked out alone.

Somehow, the petrified and bewildered sister of mine managed to scrounge some food for the hungry 'me' now and then. Papa vanished from my life for many months. That was a happy and gratifying relief, while some of my fears 'pretended' to slowly fade away. I did not know what Ethel did during all those months. We seldom saw each other, and like always we never talked.

My sister and I became close friends with the caring Papalias family. They knew of my father's despicable behavior and made a daily effort to be sure we were okay, even feeding us. Lucy and Connie Papalias were my school friends also.

There was also a beautiful Greek lady named Edith Tounger who entered my life. (Why not in Ethel's?) Edith would very often ask: "Are you hungry, Margie?" Then she and her handsome, classy husband Plato would take 'me' to the Lodi Hotel Restaurant.

We remained true friends for years until her untimely death. She died in San Francisco, the city she loved the most. She had lived just twenty minutes from 'me'.

Mama Papalias was forever kind and good, and she too was easy to love. She reminded 'me' so often of my sweet Thea. When she passed, over thirty years ago, she left her three (now adult) children, Socs, Lucy and Connie, to remain my friends. They trekked here from Lodi to one of my glorious anniversary celebrations a few years ago.

Another digression please…

My school friend Ivan of so many years ago, arranged for a bus load of our senior class from Lodi High to come to my one-woman show, "Stuff Happens and Then." What an unrivaled evening in my honor, and to see so many people, not even knowing they cared or remembered 'the me.' What a plus. After the performance, one school friend with such kindness said: "If we had known you had no place to live you could have come to live with us, no one knew."

Papa, with so much hostility, barged into our rented room late one evening, carelessly flipping twenty-five single dollar bills on a bed: "my restaurant has been sold. Stay in school. I will be back in two weeks." He never looked at us, and he never came back. "This was blatant abandonment again. We knew by now, at the beginning of our scary teenage years, just wasn't right and just wasn't the way people lived or treated one another."

This was our father's pathetic, sickness that had nothing, just nothing at all to do with his two unloved children. His sorrowful life was of his own selfish making. "Perhaps my ill begotten and irresponsible father found himself in some sort of trouble over and over. What was he escaping from? What was his peculiar and secret life all about filled with so much hatred and incalculable abuse?" To like the man who contributed to my birth, or to love him and trust him, was NOT possible. He was obviously mentally disturbed.

LIFE IS A ROLLER COASTER RIDE

Lyrics by Margie Belrose
Music by Gillian Lovejoy
Dedicated to my roller coaster life

LIFE IS A ROLLER COASTER RIDE WITH ITS
UPS AND DOWN
OOOPS EVEN FEARS AND TEARS AND LAUGHS
WITH MERRY-GO-ROUNDS AND CLOWNS
I'M GOING AND GOING UP UP UP
AND SUDDENLY DOWN DOWN DOWN
AM I READY TO FACE ALL THERE IS TO CHASE
AS I'M CIRCLING ROUND ROUND ROUND
EACH DAY THE QUESTION IS
MUST THIS RIDE BE TAKEN AGAIN
WE'VE SEEN IT BEFORE WITH RICHARD AND LIZ
WERE THEY LESSONS LEARNED IN PAIN
BUT NOT LESSONS LEARNED IN VAIN
I'M GOING AND GOING UP UP UP
AND SUDDENLY DOWN DOWN DOWN
AM I READY TO FACE ALL THERE IS TO CHASE
AS I'M CIRCLING ROUND ROUND ROUND
LIFE IS A ROLLER COASTER RIDE SWIFTLY
WHIRLING BY
LIFE IS A ROLLER COASTER RIDE
TWIRLING AND WHIRLING AM I
TWIRLING AND WHIRLING AM I
TWIRLING AND WHIRLING AM I
LIFE IS A ROLLER COASTER RIDE LIFE IS A ROLLER
COASTER RIDE WHEE

SCENE SIXTEEN

After my freshman year was miraculously over, with very little trauma, another warm season came. I couldn't wait for summer to welcome it with outstretched arms. Swimming in the inviting Lodi Lake, sunning myself and beginning to really believe (almost) that life was now a good and serene place.

By the end of the ups and downs of my first high school year, we owed ninety dollars in back rent for our small but secure room on Lockford Street, which we were told much later, was on the wrong side of the tracks, There actually were tracks fronting the rooming house.

Mr. and Mrs. Yankee, devout Seventh Day Adventists, owned this house that was safe. Mr. Yankee made his own root beer in the basement. Every Friday we were invited to join with them for a great big bottle or two of his yummy soda, while Mrs. Yankee served us a generous helping of her home made cinnamon buns. "I will never forget those special Fridays."

We did not hear from or see our formidable Papa for over three years. He made his irresponsible and planned exit at the start of my ninth grade. My sister quickly found a job as a live-in housekeeper for a wealthy family of four. Packing fruit was my solution to paying the back rent, as well as our monthly rental charge. "Where to live now? This was much too much to fathom for a kid of thirteen and a half."

Bill, who was a school friend, a very handsome heartthrob, and an athlete, implored his mother: "Can Margie stay with us for awhile? She has no place to live, she is alone."

Their kindness saved 'me' from the dreaded life on the streets that I heard so much about. Bill, his sweet Mom Allen and myself made sure we remained in touch one way or the other, and visited each other for many years after high school until they both passed away.

At that terrifying phase in my young life, Mom Allen knew a family looking for a housekeeper. That was my smart move, to the home of the Steele family. I did not know how to cook, but sure knew how to clean. The Steele home became my sheltered haven for the nine months of my tenuous sophomore year.

My squiggly life was only temporarily secure. Ten dollars a month was my grateful pay that bought 'me' two weekly dance classes at fifty cents each. I performed (oh-so-badly) in a recital, and even managed the two necessary but unattractive costumes.

I also bought a red and white sweater to excitedly go to my first football game, where I rooted with all my heart for "The Flames" as they played their guts out. "Would you believe that sweater is in my sweater drawer after all these years? It still fits and I still wear it."

The Steele's arranged for me to throw a Valentine party, for at least ten kids. We danced, listened to music and had lots of food and fun. "My first party. How good they were to 'me'!" Then, after that sheltered nine months, the two Steele children had matured enough and no longer needed my selfless help. "What to do? Where to go? Where to live?" Such burdensome and familiar terror again encircled this young teenager and my forever-disjointed life.

Ethel left her housekeeping job, and together we found a porch remodeled into a room that became our temporary mini-home. Meanwhile, we were working as waitresses. "Why would anyone hire two very young girls as waitresses? And why would anyone rent a room to two very young girls with no references or family?" Our country was at war and therefore there were no children's services or county help.

But we survived for a time. Ethel was living her secret life of impatiently looking for love; I was taking dance lessons and fantasizing about my indefinable dream, knowing it would somehow always be part of my life.

But the time came upon us to live an unwavering life. We were waitressing till eleven at night. And we had to get up by seven for school. This was not what two immature girls should or could do while still remaining out of harm's way and at least somewhat sane. Ethel was ready to enter her sophomore year and 'me' my junior. Out of sheer desperation, we put a want ad in the local paper: "Two high school girls need shelter. Will work for room and board."

A beautiful young woman of about twenty-six years old responded to the ad and came by one life changing night. We were a perfect fit and she immediately piled us with our stuff, into her car. We moved into her neat and humble home, where we were given a room with twin beds. "Oh gosh Ethel, to think this might be normal. We can be happy here; we each have our own bed and a dresser. We can be safe for now. Aren't we lucky at last? Let's be happy Ethel, we don't have to be afraid- for a while, anyway. Don't cry." This was the normal home of Marcene and Frank Ferrone and their two young children, Francene and Philip. Eventually there would be two more children, named Ferrone, Ruthie, and Todd.

Early one school morning, Ethel and I were having another yelling match. She had confiscated something of mine. Frank screamed from his bedroom (he was a screamer): "I can't stand your arguing any more! Either you both have to leave or one of you does!"

Ethel yelled back, "I'll go and I'll leave today!" And she did. I had no idea where she went on such short notice. She never told 'me'. But it was as if she had premeditated her departure and was anxious to seek out her 'secret' life of looking for that intangible element called LOVE.

My sister had a more than a difficult time with the immediate affection the Ferrones and little ole 'me' had developed. "She was never left out; but by some unexplained force, she was compelled to leave herself out."

Her incurable, ravishing envy was always on the edge of rearing it's vicious head. She never wanted to see the Ferrones again (but she did, once) and didn't want to hear about them. It was the last time we shared a mutual life or the chance to be remotely close. Which, ironically, we never had been anyway.

Very soon she found a job in the Lodi Hotel coffee shop even though she was still enrolled in school.

When she completed her sophomore year she left school for good, although she frequently denied quitting. I could not blame her for wanting to maintain her sense of worth and dignity. She hated school anyway. She continued to live somewhere. I don't know where and she never offered to tell. Her life was always so guarded, even when she seemed to be in trouble or needed help.

She managed to find a job as an operator for the phone company. A year later she moved to San Francisco. In about five years time she delivered a baby boy after a brief encounter with a sailor. She was still just a teenager.

In today's world, having a child out of wedlock would be accepted and considered typical, but at that time during the late forties, it was something to be ashamed of.

Marcene and I drove to San Francisco, retrieving her from the hospital to then settle her into a small apartment with her fatherless, beautiful, healthy newborn son.

Ethel did not recognize that this was a gesture of genuine kindness coming from Mommie Marcene's heart and reaching out willingly to touch hers. Ethel displayed no gratitude.

Having happily lived with the Ferrones only a few months, I had finally stopped biting my scrappy nails. One holiday weekend Marcene was invited to go skiing with coworkers from her high-end job at a dress shop. I don't think she even knew how to ski. But she packed so much stuff; I just knew she wasn't coming back. I began to cry inconsolably: "She isn't coming back, she isn't, and she's left for good too, like everyone else.

Daddy Frank could not comprehend what to do with such a troubled and clearly hysterical young teenager: "Margie, you have to hold tight with open arms. What you are feeling is the terrible emotion of jealousy." "What he didn't grasp was not jealousy on my part, but the all-consuming and familiar fear of abandonment."

"I am Italian and the destructive emotion of jealousy seems to run rampart in our culture. I have fought that destructive passion all my life and it can easily consume and destroy a person. Margie, learn to hold tight with open arms, as I have tried so hard to do." Those wise and worried words of Daddy Frank's have always clung tightly to 'the me'. I have attempted to live by them and have indulged my every effort to overcome such sick behavior. Jealousy does not appear to rear its' ugliness nor to be in my nature. The following is a song written about his wise advice.

HOLD TIGHT WITH OPEN ARMS

Lyrics by Margie Belrose
Dedicated to Daddy Frank

HOLD TIGHT WITH OPEN ARMS

MY PRETEND DADDY ONCE SAID

BUT ALL I COULD DO WAS CRY AND

CRY INSTEAD

SHE WILL BE BACK HE SAID

TRUST TO THAT – LET HER BE FREE

YOU'RE YOUNG SO IT IS HARD TO COMPREHEND

THAT THE NEEDS OF OTHERS

MIGHT NOT YET BE IN YOUR HEAD

JUST HOLD TIGHT WITH OPEN ARMS

WAS WHAT HE SAID

AND THOSE WERE THE WORDS

THE DADDY I LOVED SO MUCH SAID

TO THIS SCARED YOUNG CHILD

EACH NIGHT WHEN I WENT TO BED

HOLD TIGHT WITH OPEN ARMS

HOLD TIGHT WITH OPEN ARMS

AND YOUR FEARS OF HARM

WILL SOON BE GONE

HOLD TIGHT WITH OPEN ARMS MY

DEAR YOUNG ONE

SCENE SEVENTEEN

My life with a normal family held the sanctity of honesty, and I finally felt sheltered. "Surely this is what a typical family life should be!" But it was also beyond my full comprehension. The possibility was always there tweaking around 'me' that one day it would be over and the rambling life I had unhappily known would return.

My love for the sweet people who unselfishly took a castaway into their lives was immediate. I willingly cleaned their house, helped cook (although Marcene was a great cook), did laundry in her Bendix washing machine, ironed mounds and heaps of clothing (this was before no press clothes) went to school, did homework that was often beyond 'me', baby sat, and so much more: "Peace was on the tenuous edge of surrounding 'the me' at last."

I was able to join the school's tumbling team, and luckily I had a knack for it. Very soon into the daily training, my arm (I don't remember which one) was broken in a foolish but incredibly brave attempt to take a running forward dive over thirteen curled up, and possibly squeamish people.

I had seen it done before by Barbara D., the strongest girl on the team, so of course ' the me' could do it too. After that unfortunate accident I was chosen to announce the program for one of our regular Friday assemblies- this way I could still be part of the team. When this arm of mine mended, I learned lots of tumbling tricks and loved it. Of course, I was keyed up for my dance classes twice a week, and they never stopped being my priority above everything. Ethel generously mailed me a five-dollar bill for my lessons when she could.

Drama and public speaking (to help my truly wobbly knees) were the parts of my education that I looked forward to. My first two daring speeches were:

"The Abolishment of Sororities and Fraternities' and

'The Pro side of Mercy Killing."

"Isn't that a kick in the a**?" At the same time, it was reported in the local Lion's Club newspaper contest revue: "Margie Leonides stressed racial tolerance, democracy and religious tolerance through education." "What did this curious fourteen year old know? Nothing."

One of my speeches, surprisingly, received "honorable mention" in an out-of-town contest the teacher entered 'me' in. 'My' wobbly knees were now gone forever.

Oh how I wish those speeches were somewhere to be found. How interesting it would be to understand my viewpoint then as to now. It would probably be much the same. "Obviously this Margie person was ahead of her times." (Joke here).

By my eleventh year of school, I had made lots of friends at Lodi High. It was a beautiful school that was so easy to be finally comfortable in. One week, this very person writing this very book was chosen to be "Girl of the week" for the school paper, The Flame. "How could that coveted recognition come to someone like Margie Leonides, a castaway?" I even had the unmitigated pluck, by then, to try out for song leader with Joyce, another student on the tumbling team. We chose to wear the red pedal pushers we had to hastily make because neither of us had cute skirts. The senior boys didn't like that, even though we added lots of tumbling and enthusiasm. It mattered not. They wanted to see "skirts", and that turned the tide against our winning. We came in second.

On a rainy winter morning just before Daddy Frank offered to drive 'me' the eight blocks to school, the musical chimes of the doorbell rang out.

With heavy schoolbooks in hand I opened the door, and there stood a rather hunched-over man, hardly recognizable and not seen or heard from in over three years. Yes, this strange human had now drowned in his own alcoholism.

"I felt NOTHING for him, just nothing, and obviously he felt nothing for 'me'. But the question would always be: How could he still overwhelm 'me' with terror?" My body began to shake and my schoolbooks toppled to the floor. "What are you doing here? Come in and meet the Ferrones." It was impossible to call him Papa because he wasn't. Never had been, never would be. He would not come in, but instead simply said,

"I have not come to take you away again, only to say goodbye."

With that uncanny announcement, he merely turned and walked away, as was his dispassionate custom. I don't know how he knew where to find 'the me', possibly from Ethel. They managed to keep in touch through the ensuing years while both living their lives of intrigue.

After that bewildering day, he was out of my life for well over a decade. I do not remember a hug or affection from him or even talking with him. I never knew his viewpoint on anything either.

Another digression please...

What an enigma: he was basically standing there after the three years of abandonment and then dispassionately shuffled away.

The Ferrones were not the only 'make believe' folks for me to love. They also had a grandmother, Marcene's adored mother Mommie Ruth, who came into my quickly changing world. Before Ethel left the Ferrone home she did not permit any of this wonderfulness. She jealously would not allow it and could not, for reasons not even recognized by her coveted self. **"Their love would have CHANGED her life forever, as it did mine."**

My heart filled with hurt for her; she missed so much. We kept in touch the best we could through the years. Somehow she always knew where Papa was and he, her. Curiously, we never talked about him or about much of anything. Both of their lives were of many varying secrets.

During the times we did get together, she was always in a posture of self-pity about our past, breaking down a lot. She never had a cheerful outlook. Our occasional dinners failed to take us forward from the darkness she was unable to break out of. I know she tried, unintentionally, to draw 'me' into her edgy gloom. For 'the me,' it was critically necessary to not be dragged into her needy, obsessive and melancholy demeanor. "I was compelled to take a shower or wash my face when she left our few visiting times. It was emotionally necessary to bathe myself of her suffocating negative vibrations. Oh how sad. It is more than heartbreaking to relive so much of our lives."

Ethel did not want to hear about my life and the Ferrone family. "She had her own peculiar life, a life I could not envision or understand." My sister married several times with high hopes of happiness. She gave birth to two very handsome boys, and moved to Bakersfield where she worked very hard at two jobs, as a bookkeeper and a night auditor at a motel.

She was also raising her boys alone. She moved to Visalia and then to Walnut Creek, an hour distance from my world.

It seems to 'me' that her talk of embezzlement was portentously looming over her panic-stricken head, and might have influenced her decision to escape. I do not know.

My sister's weight was always a major problem once she got into her teen years, and it was effortless for her to be envious of 'me' for that **"Success together was not to be ours."** I'm sorry for that.

Mommie Ruth lived up near Sonora, California, a pretty and inviting mountain town.

The Ferrones and now lucky 'me' often took the two-hour drive there from Lodi, especially for the holidays. We traveled in Daddy Frank's exceptional black Lincoln Zephyr.

I never knew times of celebration or what they meant: the food, the laughter, the gifts, the fun, the music, and the shared love. At that extraordinary time the Ferrone conclave were a sizeable, loving family always gathering, in those years, at Mommie Ruth's to share many incomparable holidays. "This was all now part of a life that had never even been imagined by 'me'. This was a real loving family, this was sanity."

Without realizing it, they taught 'me' how to care for anyone who came into my life. Always with loving kindness, concern, sanity, and affection that will forever come out of my mouth and heart. These lessons of kindheartedness to share were the absolute promises made to myself those many years ago. Every fervent effort has been made by 'the me' to keep this dedicated vow, and I have-most of the time.

Up in the town of Sonora, just a few miles from Mommie Ruth, a summer waitressing job came my way; I rented a small room from slightly deaf Baba Burns, who looked after 'me' during that uniquely free summer. It was an unusual vacation time for work, fun, swimming, new friends, and even a short summer romance.

I earned almost four hundred dollars, and those three fun-filled months took 'me' through the whole next year of school, along with paying my summer expenses.

It covered my many dance classes, some clothes, and ventures to the movies where I breathlessly watched the incredibly talented performers. "They were my idols and forever influenced my life:" Judy Garland, Ginger Rogers, Eleanor Powell, June Alyson, Shirley Temple, Betty Hutton, Fred Astaire, Gene Kelly, Donald O'Connor, Dan Daily, Katherine Hepburn, Jimmy Durante, James Cagney, and on and on. So many. I watched them, believing all the while, **"I can do that. I will do that. I will. I will!"**

I excitedly rushed to the movies each Friday evening to watch them while squirming in my seat, wanting desperately to jump up on the stage. "But what would I do if I did get up there, Hmmmm?"

By now 'the me' lived with the Ferrones for less than two years, but it seemed so much longer, as if it had been my whole young life. My grades were never good all through school, ever since the mistake by the nuns of having 'me' skip over the third grade. Then wonder of all wonders, I caught up in my junior year while living with "my folks" "I had never said those words before, **"my folks."** Oh, they made me sound normal." With them life was stable and peaceful, and began to make common sense. Yet still, my body ached with the unforgiving terror that I had lived though in my younger years.

One February morning before school, the phone rang much too early. It was Thea's daughter, Tess, calling from far away New Jersey. Since I was writing to my Thea every few months letting her know of my whereabouts, Tess knew how to reach 'me'. The conversation went something like this: "I am remodeling my studio. Would you come here and help? You are the only person I can trust. You can finish school and take dance classes. I will pay you back the money for your ticket when you get here."

So the dilemma: "Leave the only family I'd ever known? Leave my senior year at the end of February before my June graduation? My picture had already been taken for the school yearbook. My class ring was ordered." That ring has been on my finger ever since. It is a symbol of the importance and pride I felt for myself when graduating, and reminds me of that every day.

But the chance to possibly study dancing in New York was too great a temptation. My 'folks' more than encouraged 'me'. "You must go Margie, don't be afraid, we will always remain close and write often. This could be the chance for all your fantasies to come true. You can always return. This is your home, we are your family forever, and we LOVE you." Ah, that so seldom heard word, said to 'me': "LOVE."

I took an all-too-familiar train ride, which was actually an exciting mode of travelling. I remember now that sometimes we did run away with Papa by train instead of bus. Within days I reached the slightly familiar city of Newark, New Jersey. My cousin greeted 'me' at the station and we hurriedly drove the few miles to her studio. Remembering her big dance school as the first place that my young dreams began to germinate made 'the me' anxious to see it again.

The disappointment of staring at her former studio that was now being remodeled into a Fred Astaire ballroom franchise, with miniature rooms sharing the once large space, caused my heart to break. Tess had lied and caustically betrayed 'the me'. This behavior was her norm with everyone, I later learned. Could never go back and I don't remember seeing her there again. In thinking about her phone conversation, she clearly said, "You are the only person I can trust." What an irony. I had to look for a high school somewhere and made unrealistic plans to return to California.

Tess never paid back the money that Daddy Frank had lent 'me' for the sorry trip there. As a wedding gift years later, he forgave the several hundred-dollar debt.

"So, off to live with Thea again – but what to really do?"

I felt deceived and resentful about Tess's lies and deliberate betrayal. My dear Thea had no answers for 'me'. I suspect she sadly realized her daughter could not be trusted. It was and is beyond 'me' to comprehend the peculiar reason for her trickery, to this very day.

Let's call this an intermission, if you will,
And then we'll stroll into Act 2
We should take a break from our stroll
Have some water or better yet
A cold glass of Pinot Grigio.
There will be a few pictures to gaze.
For some people mentioned in our stroll,
no pictures could be found and some of those found
I do not know where they came from.
Possibly when I received an envelope in the mail
In my early twenties
with some pictures and my birth certificate.
Maybe now is the time to go to the rest room
And then ON WITH OUR STROLL

Sophie and Harry
(two unidentified gentlemen behind)

A father I never knew like this

Saint Vincents's Home, Saginaw, Michigan

Saint Vincents's Home, Saginaw, Michigan

Girls' Dining Room

NOT

Sister Theresa

Who??

Swimming Pool Fun

Saint Vincents's Villa,
Saginaw, Michigan

PROTESTANT ORPHAN ASYLUM
988 JEFFERSON AVENUE, DETROIT MICHIGAN
CORNER STONE LAID JUNE 15, 1891
DEDICATED OCTOBER 13, 1892

Lodi High School, 1947

The Trinity Lutheran Church
as it once was ...

... and as it stands today
As The Belrose

Ethel

My Thea

Paul & Ethel O'Brien   *Cousin Victoria*

Various ages of myself, do not know my age in most

Ethel and me at St. Vincent's
We must have been around
8 and 9 years old

Behind my Thea's Restaurant
in Elizabeth Port

Lodi Lake about 16 years old

A favorite
picture of myself

Senior Prom

Graduation

*I was 18 and won
a photo contest*

*Mommie Marcene and
me about 18 yrs old*

*In the studio when
I first met David*

*Having fun at
Santa Monica Beach*

Our Wedding Day
March 15, 1953

Pat and Stanley Kahn, Mommie Marcene,
David, Margie, Daddy Frank

David

David when I first met him

D. Belrose

kappa delta pi

Kappa Delta Pi is a national education honorary fraternity. It is composed of members who have shown outstanding ability in this field.

A high fraternity award

DAVID & ME   our first show here, 1963

He was a funny, thinking man

Teaching Classes

Davy and Dea

*Should I shoot my mommie
or hug my doll*

Davy and myself

Dea Performing

They protected each other always

Me, Davy and Dea
6 months after David left this world

Our family at it's happiest '68
David, Dea, Davy, Me
and Sweet Nanette

Davy stuck a finger in his eye, Dea sucked her thumb

Oh how I've loved performing

Davida

Sue Sue

Robert Micheli

Wilfred George

Norma Machad

*David's Band
The Baltimore
Steam Packet
with Davy, myself
and Dea for our schools
50th anniversary*

*Ken Vix and myself
for our schools 50th*

Charlie

1996 Marin Women's Hall of Fame

Yes, I do love animals

A horse I got to ride

Nanny poo and me
in a self portrait

Beautiful Purly Mae

Loving Rosie ...

... and now Binky

Act 2
SCENE EIGHTEEN

Within a few weeks of being welcomed again at my Thea's, a phone call came from my unknown half sister.

To recharge your memory, she was the child that Sophie and Harry had conceived when Sophie deserted us, the child she later gave birth to in prison.

I could not believe that same young girl was now talking to 'me' on the phone. Keep in mind several things:

I had met Sophie for the first time when Ethel lived with her and our half sister as an eleven year old. That was the first time I had actually met my supposed mother and she had beaten me fiercely, all because I was innocently tapping my little ten-year-old feet to the music on the radio. I never met my half sister that day of bleakness.

Still recapping: the second time I saw her a few months later, Sophie was forcing Ethel to stumble for at least five miles, while Sophie rode comfortably in a cab to Thea's house. Then, in another fit of manic rage, she beat 'me' again. "Oh such overwhelming sad memories. I promise not to cry."

"We would like to invite you to dinner on Sunday," this stranger of a relative told me. In my shock, I could only mumble, "I'm not sure, but I will let you know." "How did this odd grapevine work? How did they even know of my whereabouts?" Suspicious of it all, I had to talk it over with my Thea: "Margie, go and meet her on Sunday. Try to keep an open mind."

Oh I did not want to go. My gut feeling screamed: "Don't,

Margie! But try to keep an open mind." I did visit them that black Sunday and in telling them of Tess's betrayal they suggested: "Come live with us while you finish out your senior year." Again, I went back to Thea for advice. She said, "Give her a chance. She was just a young girl when she married your Papa. She is older now, and maybe she can be a good mother this time." All of this said in her charming Greek accent, which I can still hear in my ears to this day.

"Thea, the two times we met, she beat 'me'. I don't know or like her. She is mean and has a violent temper that can instantly explode for no reason. I just can't do this." But nevertheless, I took Thea's tolerant advice and went into an anonymous and demoralizing family that consisted of a half brother, a sister, a man I would never come to know, and a woman who did not like 'me'. Those feelings were made mutual all too soon. These new circumstances set 'me' into mental as well as a physical turmoil, and I consider it an ill-fated decision on my part.

This new 'sister' Francis was a person I honestly did make an effort to know. However, she was very unlike 'me', and we soon discovered that we had absolutely nothing in common. In later years, with all good intentions, we tried to have a letter writing relationship. Even one visit by her to California. It was not successful, in fact it was a disaster.

I enrolled at a high school in Roselle, New Jersey, which was near their home. I attempted to tolerate this strange family; I had not been able to see clearly just how awful they were on that first black Sunday. By this time, because of my serene life in Lodi, I had lived and knew what 'normal' and sane was.

I never called Sophie "mother." As a matter of fact, I could not address her as anything. It did not take long to know, really know, this was a mistake that went beyond dreadful. My very being felt consumed by this inescapable hell, and I was filled with fresh waves of relentless fear. I could not grasp what cruel happenings would be thrust upon this Margie person next. Needless to say, it could not last long. Again the question: "What to do?"

I saw her obedient and spineless husband Harry only once, and we rarely exchanged words. He worked long hours in a diner he owned a few miles from their home. Harry Gallos could not help but continue submitting to Sophie's vile demands, and would tirelessly wait for his nightly reward.

I felt tricked again, this time by the whole detestable Gallos family. As it turned out, there was no bed to call my own and I was obliged to share one with Frances. They all squatted in an unattractive and depressing basement, with barely enough of their ugly furniture. The upstairs was beautifully furnished in expensive French provincial. It was nuts.

This was a living area that was never lived in, however; it was supposed to be cleaned every week, including a tiled kitchen with brand new appliances. The kitchen was never used. It seemed crazy and unnatural, "No, it was crazy and unnatural and oddly enough, seemed like a punitive atmosphere."

Sophie never stopped secretly reading trashy romance magazines, and fooling herself into believing she was effectively hiding her lifelong cigarette addiction from her obedient servant of a husband. If the T.V. soap operas of today where on back then, she probably would have spent her days vicariously living them also. "I watched, those two months there, but did not see her ever make a stab at a happy, normal or productive life of her own. Who was she?"

She would at times jump off her very used and smelly dilapidated couch, with little or no reason, and would run screaming after her teenage son. (The half brother I didn't even know or talk to at that time).

She had unreasonable outbursts, while viciously beating him with whatever was on hand. Eventually he would find a way to escape from her wrath and out any door or window he could reach. I heard later through that same grapevine that John, in his early twenties, had developed into a disturbed young man with many evil faces: i.e. stealing, forging, lying, trickery, scamming. He learned this appalling behavior from someone; I leave it to you, dear reader, to decide whom.

Sophie was without a doubt, a seriously unstable woman. She read my mail, going through my two pathetic drawers every day. One afternoon, with trepidation, I asked for permission and money to go to New York to study dance once a week. She simply said NO and actually turned her back, with no explanation. This was possibly my only real New York chance, puff, just gone. If she had said yes, perhaps there could have been some scrap of forgiveness in my heart for the years of abandonment and abuse.

I faithfully sent weekly letters to the Ferrone family, and they in turn wrote back. I still have all their letters. Sophie could not resist the impulse to snoop into my meager belongings and forage thru my private box of personal things and read their letters. She was unbelievably jealous, even going so far as to cruelly scream out, "You and that woman are "queer!" This sick, jealous, caustic birth mother and my unfortunate, envious sister Ethel must have been of the same disparaging cut. I never understood the insane jealousy that neither one of them could control and viciously exuded what must be called 'hate'.

SCENE NINETEEN

However, this new but familiar foreboding life was not totally glum. In this negative environment there was some fun- not in their dysfunctional, hateful, unnerving home, but at my new high school.

I was very popular, and everyone knew me as that senior student from California. Fellow students were star struck: "Gosh, you must know all the movie stars. What's California like?" They would laugh at what they called my California accent, but in fact they were the ones with a strong New Jersey accent.

Many dates came my way. I went to the class picnic, to fun day, then to the junior and senior proms with the most handsome boy in the senior class, "Fuzzy" Richard Brueckner, As well as the class president. (Fuzzy and I are still in touch after all these years). It was cool, as they say these days, and Sophie did pony up to buy 'the me' a pretty prom dress

A small digression again, please.

The way that diseased family lived and spent their lives was unnecessary, Harry had a successful diner and they indeed had money. There was no understandable reason to live in such an ugly squalor of a basement while all else was quite lovely and comfortable looking. It was crazy.

School was something to look forward to every day; it was my temporary escape from an unloving and harsh family that 'the me' was so grateful not to be a permanent member of. This bedraggled life only lasted for maybe eight weeks.

When I had completed high school, I found a job with the phone company and intended to save up enough to fly back to California. My graduation occurred in Roselle, New Jersey, but I have always felt like a Lodi High graduate. After all, my dismal time in New Jersey that I was frenetically trying to flee from lasted actually only a short time. Meanwhile my happy, safe and sane time in Lodi had spanned nearly four years.

After completing my years of education and all during that quirky transitional period of time, Mommie Marcene took a plane to Virginia to see her two sisters. My telephone supervisor permitted 'me' to take two days off to visit her. When I returned that third day, sometime before six in the morning, Fuzzy picked 'me' up at the small airport. When I arrived back, I rang their side doorbell and Harry, not Sophie, abruptly opened the door. Out of his mouth he immediately vomited poisonous verbal venom. This no doubt had been instigated by the godless coward he called his wife. She was most likely cornered up in her usual depressing and dark bedroom that was more like a foreboding cave.

Harry could not help but bend to her slavish demands as he had done for years, no matter right or wrong, good or bad. He was powerless and knew no other way to live. Among his nasty words, the last thing he said and most likely the only thing I remember him ever saying: "You're not welcome here, don't come in and don't come back." He slammed the door in my stunned face.

All my paltry belongings, minus the prom dress and the graduation gift of a cheap watch, were in a junk heap in their driveway, lying by his new green Hudson car.

Fuzzy helped gather my pathetic things and drove the bewildered 'me' to my equally bewildered Thea. It was evident that the Gallos family, by their own miserable design, lived their pitiful lives in a murky black environment **completely devoid of even a breath of joy, goodness or kindness.** It was a world that Margie Leonides was miraculously saved from, so many eons before.

I Never saw or heard from Sophie

ever again FOR THE REST OF MY LIFE

And this was a blessing for 'the me'

A small digression again, please.

Here are some odd thoughts to be contemplated about Sophie:

"What did her handwriting look like? Was she right or left-handed? Were there grandparents somewhere? What did she do besides read her coveted magazines? Did she drive? Did she have friends? What did her body look like? What did her hands look like? Did she have fun? Did she have any hobbies? Did she go to the movies? Did she go to a beauty salon? How big were her feet? Was she educated? I knew her screaming, not her laughter. I knew her unlikeable face with always a frown. I did not know her smile.

Where were the brother and sister she traveled to America with? When was her birthday? Was she so embroiled in her blatantly unpleasant disposition that she could not be happy? Was she a loving mother to her two other children?

I do not know anything about her at all; only the disturbed woman with a demeaning, out-of-control, and horrendous temper. And she knew nothing of these things about 'me' or Ethel. I think at one time she might have been pretty, before evil enveloped her countenance."

Again, so many unanswered questions, such an ongoing quandary. I barely knew her for a few intolerable months of my life and am GRATEFUL that such a hateful and unstable woman never raised 'me,' and I am GRATEFUL the formidable, equally hateful and unstable man never raised 'me'. It may seem untrue, but goodness has somehow tracked and guided 'me'. The only lesson those two pitiless and violent people taught 'me' was **WHAT NOT TO BE**.

The abnormal people in the menacing Gallos household were as easy for 'me' to dismiss as I was for them. "I believe hate is a discernible emotion, but indifference is far worse because it equals a 'nothing'. Indifference, in this case in point, became the morose emotion stemming from the apathetic relationship of Sophie, her husband, two children and consequently 'the me'.

Is there forgiveness for them?" I would like there to be, but don't know, at least for now. Maybe when "The Me I Found" comes to the end of this ongoing and upward chronicle, there will be some pardon, if only just a smattering.

After deftly taking a city bus to live again with Thea for a few months, I scrimped together enough money from my phone company employment to make a joyful return to California and the Ferrone family. "It took me a long time to believe and say "my family," They had, by this time, moved from Lodi to a city near Santa Cruz, California, to a better paying situation Daddy Frank had procured in his profession as a CPA.

I know their four kids to this day and love them. They will always be my family. Life finally became stable because of that exceptional family and their wise influence. My very own spiritual guides surely have been there from the day of my arrival into this wacky world of nonstop fear and dark confusion, from the time of irresponsible abandonment and to this very day, and forever more. "Is this all FORTUNATE? YES."

Without that family, MY family, I cannot wildly imagine what my life might have turned out to be."

Upon my exciting return, when not yet attaining eighteen years of age and stupidly acting like a "know-it-all", it would turn out very quickly that the things I did then were based on blameless and immature thinking. How naïve and ignorant this person called 'me' really was in my new eighteen years of age.

In spite of all the dumb things said and done at that transitional time of my life, I found a secretarial job though I could barely type. I was earning a living, paid my few bills, felt independent, bought a little used car, and too quickly entered a relationship that had no chance of succeeding. Mommie Marcene taught me to drive that little car, thru the hills around Santa Cruz. And so a warm feeling of peace was beginning to engulf 'the me' as it had before when first living with "my family" in Lodi. At that time, the small farm town of Lodi almost began to feel like it was my 'hometown'.

I was now free of so many incalculable uncertainties:

❀ Free of a father I never really knew or liked, a father who was evil and so volatile he made life uncertain and tenuous even when he was nowhere in sight. Was he mentally disturbed? It would seem so, he had to be.

❀ Free of my forever complicated, sad and embittered sister who loved 'me', hated 'me', needed 'me', lied to 'me', stole from 'me', hurt 'me', fought with 'me', and was proud of 'me' but also jealous of 'me'. I loved her, of course, but it was very difficult to like her.

 Free of Sister Mary Matthew the terrible, and her vicious attacks that were unwarranted, malicious, evil and humiliating. The remembered punitive acts have never seemed to completely leave my susceptible and tender psyche.

 Free of Sophie the tyrant, who as a thoughtless girl of eighteen gave 'me' life but was totally incapable of love or compassion, and who was never a mother to 'me'. She was callous, cruel, and self-absorbed, showing only the jealous, mean, erupting temper and selfish, narcissistic side of her truly distraught nature. In conclusion, "She was not a nice person."

Writing most of these experiences down that made up my incoherent life begs the question, "Am I really free?"

These shadowy emotions smolder into my memory and into my solemn soul, into THE ME I am besieged to find.

"Will the writing of this book do that for 'me'?"

Call, I'll let you know.

415-454-6422

ON A SUMMER AFTERNOON

Lyrics by Margie Belrose
Music by Gillian Lovejoy
Dedicated to the future I was looking for

ON A SUMMER AFTERNOON WHEN I TURNED SEVENTEEN

MY LIFE WAS GLORIOUSLY BEFORE ME

I WAS TRANSPORTED TO A LIFE I NEVER DREAMED

WHAT SHOULD I DO BUT LET THIS DREAM ALLURE ME

THOUGH THE YEARS HAVE GONE BY STILL I OFTEN TRY

TO REMEMBER THAT SUMMER IN JULY

WHEN MY LIFE WAS GLORIOUSLY BEFORE ME

COULD IT BE TRUE THAT I WAS UNAWARE

TO NEVER SEE THE ME THAT LONGED TO BE SET FREE

TO NEVER REALIZE THE PROMISE THERE

THAT SUMMER AFTERNOON WHEN I JUST TURNED

SEVENTEEN

WHEN I LONGED TO BE SET FREE, TO BE SET FREE

A LIFETIME AGO

Lyrics and Music by Margie Belrose
Arranger, Gillian Lovejoy
Dedicated to a life 'the me' escaped from

IS IT POSSIBLE THAT THE HURT AND SORROW

OF A LIFETIME AGO HAS

NOW BECOME BEARABLE?

IS THIS SWEET JOY THAT I NOW FEEL?

THOUGH IT HAS TAKEN YEARS OF PAIN

AND MUCH MORE I CAN'T EXPLAIN

(BRIDGE)

I AM FREE AT LAST – SADNESS NO MORE

HURT AND PAIN HAS FLOWN FROM MY SOUL

IT WAS JUST A LIFETIME AGO, A LIFETIME AGO

A LIFETIME AGO

I GO ON BECAUSE IT REALLY HASN'T BEEN

THAT LONG

THE TIMES HAVE CHANGED AND NOW I KNOW

IT WAS REALLY JUST A LIFETIME AGO

WHAT HAS COME AND GONE IS WHAT I RECALL

IN THE DARK OF THE NIGHT

WHEN SLUMBER TAKES MY ALL

I KNOW IT REALLY WAS BUT A LIFETIME A JUST

A LIFETIME AGO JUST A LIFETIME AGO

© 2009 Margie Belrose

SCENE TWENTY

On a desolate cloudy day I found myself in a temporary depression that resulted in a crying jag on Mommie Marcene's giving shoulders. It was mostly concerning a short but intense relationship that I had to drop a final curtain on. But more importantly, it was about my frustration at not finding the right path to forge my life-long goal to even start, let alone attain my elusive dream: "to be a DANCER."

My lengthy, sought-after aspiration was not to be famous (well that would have been nice) or to be "out there." I just wanted to spend my life dancing, and to dance well with every day surrounded by boundless JOY. Mommie Marcene advised: "If you really want your life long vision to come true, Margie, move to San Francisco, where you can study with professional teachers."

I will never know what inspired 'me' to find and go to the Capezio Dancewear store on Market Street in San Francisco. I asked for the help and advice of owners, Ethel and Paul O'Brien. "Please direct 'me' where to go for the professional training I am desperate for." That kind couple took 'me' into their generous hearts. 'Me' being a young, eager, and innocent potential. In a very short time, we became dear and lasting friends, always being outgoing with their advice.

They directed 'me' to the Mason-Kahn Studio on Market Street. It was a perfect, professional school where I could begin the training that was to develop 'me' into the dancer I longed to become. Watching Ethel O'Brien in her business dealings with customers, the example I watched and hungrily gobbled in was: "how absolutely straightforward she was!" It became a lesson I practice today, and one taught to my children to live by.

However in my life, I have so often observed there are those who don't, don't, want to, or cannot, understand straight-forwardness and honesty. "Thank you Ethel and Paul O'Brien with all my heart, for such a valuable life lesson you unknowingly taught the vulnerable 'me'." George Orwell wrote: "In times of universal deceit telling the truth becomes a revolutionary act." Food for thought I would say.

I took their guidance seriously, and early every Tuesday morning for many weeks, no matter the weather, I drove my very own cute little blue '39 Plymouth Coupe to San Francisco. There, I would take a half-hour private lesson with a knowledgeable and highly respected dancer and teacher, Stanley Kahn, who taught alongside his wife Pat Mason.

It was almost two hours of travelling for my anticipated half-hour lesson and then two hours back. I would, however, stop to visit my friend Edith and her husband Plato, in their Third Street bar, for an hour or so.

"You can see this ridiculous commute could not last very long. More than just a thirty-minute weekly lesson was necessary to reach my life's goal." There were no freeways then, only two-way highways. On both sides of the road there were beautiful fruit orchards, and yes, it was a sumptuous commute, but an impossible weekly trip.

SCENE TWENTY-ONE

In my mind, it was now vital to move to San Francisco. Since the Papalias family had already moved there, Mama invited 'me' to live with them till I could situate myself.

After a few start-and-stop jobs and many interviews, a secretarial job was offered to 'me'. (By this time 'the me' had become a pretty good typist).

So my dance classes with Mr. Kahn and Miss Pat began, every weekday evening and every Saturday, I was filled with a fervor that was hard to control.

I rushed by bus to the S.F. Ballet twice weekly to study with Harold Christenson or his wife, Ruby Asquith, in their Washington Street studios. Then I would scramble onto another city bus to get to the Greg Moore Ballroom Studio for a stimulating private lesson with David Belrose. (Sparks were soon sparking). Soon, I had to make the essential move from Mama's home that was way up Geary Blvd. almost near the ocean, to the Evangeline Hotel for Women on Seventh and McAllister Street.

This safe and sound hotel was next door to the President Follies, a burlesque house. What an absolute joy. A hotel for women run by the Salvation Army, next door to a burlesque house. Loved it. One night while walking by the 'house', from my lesson, I overheard a mother telling her ambitious daughter as they hurried to the backstage entrance: "This is a great opportunity, darling, make the best of it."

The move made it possible to be nearer to my secretarial job and to the studios I could not help but skip to for six days a week. (From five thirty to at least ten p.m.. on weekdays, Saturdays from ten a.m. to eight p.m.).

"Was this heaven? YES. Was I almost too tired to get to work? Yes, but, no matter, it was my fantasy. Falling asleep during my lunch break under my oak desk while resting my weary head on a tiny purple satin pillow was a daily reprieve."

My secretarial job earned 'me' two hundred and seventy-five dollars a month. Two hundred dollars were for classes, seventy-five were for living, and not a penny was left over. My skimpy budget from those days of seeing my unrealistic vision struggling to burst forth is still tucked among my many sentimental treasures. It mattered not that crackers and strawberry jam became my lunch and dinner at times. The Khans would often treat 'me' to a late supper at their favorite Chinese restaurant.

When the city bus fare was raised by only five cents, I had to run, scrounge or beg a ride from any thoughtful person around. "Imagine that, just a nickel."

The Ferrones, soon after my move to San Francisco, left each other after their eighteen-year marriage and four children.

Mommie Marcene ended up moving to different places, even Alaska (where I went to visit her once), marrying a few times. Daddy Frank remarried also, but continued to live near Santa Cruz. It was imperative that we all kept in touch.

One Sunday afternoon, I took a nervous two-hour drive to Daddy Frank's home near Santa Cruz, to simply thank him for his kind words of advice and guidance on that hysterical night of mine so many years ago. The 'me' stayed overnight, catching up and meeting his new wife, who was no longer 'new', as they had been married many years, by this time.

Despite the Ferrones' many years of separate lives, they both passed away within a few months of each other. I cannot quite get over the loss: " How could I? How could I?"

I WILL ALWAYS THINK OF THEM WITH LOVING GRATITUDE.

I murmur "thank you" every morning with warm tears that try to keep spilling out of my eyes. "Thank you Mommie Marcene and Daddy Frank for my life, showing and teaching 'me' love, kindness, and what is normal."

SCENE TWENTY-THREE

Being a beginner's teacher on Saturdays was part of my perpetual life-long ambition that was miraculously almost about to bloom.

Following several years of zealous and diligent training, Mr. Kahn kindly advised: "You really cannot be a professional dancer, Margie, because five foot two is just too short these days." About the same time, Harold Christenson from the S.F. Ballet with much concern, also announced: "Margie, you will not become a professional ballet dancer because you have to be at least five foot five, and you do not have the god-given gift of a classical turnout, and it is a gift."

Distressing devastation and disappointment captured my all completely, for several disparaging weeks: "If a professional life is not for 'me,' then being a teacher will be my answer. Someone has to teach. Yep, I'll do that and will be dancing at least. Teaching could kind of fulfill my dance aspirations. Maybe not exactly, but dancing will certainly be my life's work."

So, I would and could do that. My training for the next few years had to now make a turn around and would be diligently focused on becoming a really good teacher of tap, jazz, ballet and ballroom. That became my determined ambition."

Got to jump ahead right here. (You'll catch on).

(I love these curly cues)

On March fifteen, 1953, a beautiful Sunday afternoon, Dr. Dan Custer of the Science of Mind Church performed our marriage ceremony: the joining of David and Margie.

Mommie Marcene, Daddy Frank (they had not left each other yet), and Mommie Ruth came to our small wedding in the Shakespeare Garden of Roses in Golden Gate Park, along with other friends and co-workers. We were the first couple to ever marry in Golden Gate Park, as far as was known to that point. Stanley and Pat Kahn stood up for us at our wedding. They insisted we borrow their car for our three-day honeymoon up the Russian River.

We were awe struck to see the home of Jack London, who happened to be David's idol. We watched his widow going from one dwelling to another on their property. She was wearing a long black dress and carrying a pail. We even sat on their fence soaking in such an unusual experience. This before the London home became a national park.

Mr. Kahn and Miss Pat also prepared a pre-wedding dinner in their lovely home the night before, and a wedding brunch topped off with a case of champagne: It was more than magnificent. We kept one bottle for many years, opening it when we bought our building, which will be told later as we continue our bumpy stroll hand in hand.

David didn't set out to be my teacher of life, but he did become my teacher in countless other ways, most importantly:

"He taught 'me' to think logically – not just emotionally, which had always been my tendency. I knew how to cry, yes, to be scared, yes, to have fear overtake 'me' every day, yes, to be lonely, alone and unloved, yes, etc., etc., etc. But to think, to figure things out, NO, never knew that logic."

I need to talk a little of David's life, before 'me', so you will understand why we probably should not have taken the serious plunge into marriage.

He was born and grew up in East St. Louis, a tough place even today. His mother, Mary, passed away when he was two. His father, David, tried to raise him up alone. Fortunately, there were relatives nearby who helped bring up the unhappy, lonely and motherless child. David's father remarried several times. His third marriage took hold, but his wife Esther decided they needed to rid themselves of a very young, and possibly troublesome, David.

One afternoon the lonely boy over heard his stepmother pleading, "Please put your son in an orphanage so we can build our own lives." (Oh, dear, this does sound heartlessly familiar). But David's father wisely refused. However, the soon to be grown up David remembered those unkind words and could not forget them. He enlisted in the Navy the very day he turned seventeen, for a four-year stint.

It was his escape from a stepmother who didn't want, know, or love him, and a confused father trapped in the agonizing middle. Esther by then started her own family with David's father.

David's young enlistment sent him to the South Pacific during World War two, where he saw some combat as a radioman. When his recruitment in the Navy was completed he settled in San Francisco and found himself, all too quickly, in a few short-term but serious love relationships. At the same time, he held a government security job as a cryptographer.

After a year, he left his secure job and enrolled at San Jose State to study psychology, philosophy and English.

In the Navy he discovered the English language and how the words should really sound. Coming from St. Louis, he heard only the harsh accent full of dees, days, dos and dems. His new educated way of speaking now sounded very different and he liked it. "No, he fell in love with the English language."

David transferred to San Francisco State with over a 4.2 average. When tested in the Navy, his superiors were in amazement when informing him of his high, genius IQ. Another reason we should not have married: "You see, never knew my IQ. Never went to college (oh, a few extension classes) and am not an intellectual, just a dancer and performer." "One time an uninformed man caustically blurted out to 'me': "Dancers have their brains in their feet."(At least he didn't say, "up their a**")."

David: could not emotionally bring himself to resume his life in St. Louis after the Navy. He never saw his father again: "Did he regret that? Yes. Did he grieve over it? Yes? Did he wish he had been psychologically strong enough to see his father at least once again? Yes."

When he reluctantly phoned his father after many years of neglect on both their parts, he felt he was in a deep need to talk to him, to reconnect. David was casually told by Esther of his father's early death as the result of a fatal heart attack. Dejected David wilted into a state of depression and unforgiving regrets that hung on for months.

David did not complete his college endeavors, though he pursued them off and on for over seven years. His downfall in this complicated area of his life was that he simply refused to study subjects he wasn't interested in. He knew the game, but foolishly refused to play it, to his own detriment. He was his own person, albeit, possibly his own worst enemy. Though he was disciplined in many ways, it was near to impossible for him to follow a planned schedule of any kind with concerted and regimented effort and direction. This was difficult for 'me' to abide as my nature has always been the exact opposite.

Although he intellectually had IT, something inside his complex psyche prevented him from accomplishing the 'stuff' he yearned to do and could do. His life always seemed to be an agonizing question he was powerless to grapple with or tackle, even on his best days. "Yes, he was a plagued man, knowing of his high intellect but believing he could not live up to it in his own mind, even though he excelled in everything he tried and did. He never failed." He did not seem to recognize his exceptional god-given talents.

Before we met, and early into our relationship, David drifted into a few jobs after his government work, none to his liking, but discovered along his own bumpy way that he was a good ballroom dancer and had a knack for choreography and teaching. And this brings us back to our meeting.

In 1951, I walked into the Greg Moore Ballroom studio on Geary Blvd. in San Francisco. It was to be an evening that would miraculously twist and change our lives forever.

There stood a man who looked very much like the handsome movie actor, the late Edmond O'Brien. David moved, as a dancer must, with style, grace and charm. He became my ballroom teacher. He became my teacher. "He was almost too easy to fall in love with."

SCENE TWENTY-FOUR

After our courtship of over a year resulting in marriage, we rented a charming apartment on Chestnut Street in San Francisco (later to a more affordable one, in knotty pine décor on Douglas Street).

Our lives consisted of scurrying back and forth to work, studying and then teaching numerous dance classes, but not earning much money. We were continually working out a convoluted time schedule and an even more scrammy money budget. Somehow we made tender love in between all the chaos, "I must admit, chaos of our own design." But we never deterred in our unrelenting efforts to find the mysterious method to make this undefined concept called "a marriage" work.

It was near to impossible with our somewhat similar backgrounds. There were many unforeseen problems that we thought were not solvable, and some that we never were able to muddle through.

David was a Virgo, but contrary to that heavenly sign, he was indeed an incorrigible procrastinator. "It drove 'me' nuts."

Money was always elusive, which didn't help unravel our thorny situation. We separated several times, but furtively tiptoed back, always trying, trying, trying to come to grips with what we deemed as our own exclusive problems.

We diligently struggled to make sense out of things, and that would by some phenomenon guide us into a life of happiness and harmony.

We did love each other, and always would, no matter what, and there were numerous "no matter what's" during our eighteen years of up-and-down togetherness.

With so much of this miss-mosh barely behind us, the time came sooner than planned when in 1954; we opened our long-anticipated school of dance.

Of course, neither one of us had family roots, so it mattered not where we would ultimately land.

By this time David had given up his dream of possibly continuing his studies to ultimately find a career as a clinical psychologist. This was probably an unspoken lifelong regret of his. However, my own enduring dream finally became our ambition, 'in concert '. We looked for a situation to carry out our dance studio plans, going first to the south of San Francisco, then north, and finally to a sleepy town called San Rafael, California. It was an anxious quest of looking for a studio space that would strike us as right. And we did find it.

"Mr. Pierce we have only one hundred and forty dollars. We would like to rent the suite in the rear of your building. We do not have the last month's rent, nor a deposit, and we need a three year lease." We could see he was obviously aghast at such a presumption coming out of my young, inexperienced mouth. In less than an hour, however, we struck an equitable arrangement.

On a warm California day July of 1954, we bravely opened the doors of a dance school that was, by this time, our shared dream come true. This new life was a never-ending financial wrangle, but a happy tussle in limitless other ways. After all we were…

DANCING, TEACHING, ESTABLISHING A PROFESSIONAL LIFE

We named our first studio: "The Belrose Dance Workshop."

In the meantime, we moved from San Francisco to the picturesque town of Mill Valley, into an equally picturesque small house in the hills.

We were young, content, untested, and happiness was brilliantly staring us in our willing and raring-to-go faces.

So what was said, by 'me', one momentous, moonlit night, might seem foolish, even irresponsible, since we had opened our studio less than a year: "David, let's make a baby tonight." And we did, on that very romantic moonlit night.

"It can only be explained that my hormones must have been in a wild impetuous rage."

Two years before that fabulous, life-changing night, a very real nighttime dream came to 'me' within the first two weeks of our young marriage. The dream was an image of a lovely little girl standing right there, not as an infant, but rather like a two-year-old, with long brown hair and blue eyes: "What is your name, little girl?"

"My name is Dea Belrose." So, of course when our first-born was to enter this bewildering world, naturally it had to be a little girl. Everything was pink, and the talk was always, "When Dea gets here."

Our new first baby arrived. "It's a boy."

"No, doctor, it can't be; it is suppose be a little girl, that's the plan. Please look again." Dr. McCann, with controlled patience, said, "It's a healthy boy Margie, be happy."

In fact, while anxious to cuddle this long, slender, five-pound six-ounce child in my arms, I asked of myself over and over, "How is it possible to love anyone or anything else like this again?" Taking my wise doctor's advice, I was overwhelmed with happiness—an emotion that had never been experienced in my life before. Holding this new child, David John Belrose II, it was only natural to lovingly fuss over him with all the baby talk and cooing that had never been showered upon 'me' in my own infant life.

The evening before this first creature of pure delight was to be born onto a planet that would surely shine happiness on him, a lifelong friend, Ken Vix, and I were lightly playing tennis: "Oops, it is time to rush to the hospital, Ken."

Labor lasted many painful hours, (as you mommies reading this memoir know only too well), with lifelong Ken and husband David hovering close by, but impatiently pacing the hallways. Dr. McCann would saunter in often, asking, "Do you want anything to ease the pain?"

"No doctor, this is my time to be courageous, but did your wife ever take anything for the birth of your four children?"

He didn't hesitate. "Yes."

"Then bring it on." At last, Davy finally and cautiously peeked through, from a warm and safe place he shared with no one for nine months:

"I'm here at last. Sorry I had to hurt you my Hony Mom in the many hours of struggling through the birth canal to get here. I know you wanted your girl, Dea, but you've got me, your planned baby. I'll make you happy and be your hero, promise, with all my heart."

After Davy's arrival we moved to San Rafael. Even the short drive from Mill Valley was too much with a delicate little one, and our blossoming year-old school, which was slowly growing.

Two years later, on the night our unexpected second child was to look into the unknown: "David, it's time to get to the hospital."

He got up, showered, shaved, and dressed, all done slowly, as was his style, "Please hurry, it's time."

"We've lots of time, remember how long it took for Davy."

We finally left. He started to turn right. "No, David, turn left."

With great speed by then, we pushed through the hospital doors. I was immediately put in a wheelchair, when the nurse cried out: "Oh, my God, the baby is coming." They quickly tucked 'me' in bed just painless moments before that five-pound little sweetheart, Dea Marcene Belrose, made her first squeak. The doctor could not wait to happily announce: "It's a girl."

What a glorious and long-awaited declaration. Without skipping a beat, Dea sang out: "Hello world, I'm here at last and I'm gonna spend my life dancing with my hony mom."

"Thank you, thank you, Dr. McCann." As if he had anything at all to do with this brand new cherub being a girl.

David, in a braggadocios attitude, cock-stepped through the hospital hallways to broadcast to anyone willing to listen of his personal achievement. As if he alone was responsible for this new pink, wiggly-toed thing being the long awaited precious girl. "Oh, who cares? We have a precocious son and now a marvel to behold, a little daughter. What could be sweeter? Could we have planned it better ourselves? We are a family." My ardent promise then and there was:

"We will always be a kind and loving family always, **and we truly are.**"

SCENE TWENTY-FIVE

We taught dance for three years in our pink studio in the Pierce Building, furnished with wrought iron, sweetheart-shaped ice cream tables and chairs, big mirrors, and long ballet bars. Our lease was up, and we were forced to make a hard decision. "What shall we do David, continue our efforts, or not? And if we don't, what direction should we take our lives? I know you can always work for the government again."

Shortly after, we made a couple of temporary moves with no place to teach. Then by chance we moved to a house a few blocks from our Pierce Building studio. David cleverly turned a portion of the house into a small teaching area, as well as very cramped living quarters. Difficult financial straits continued to nag us with no kind let up (and they always have).

In 1958, living in the house that David turned into our studio and home, and the year Dea miraculously arrived, it was the year our beloved country of America was going through a difficult recession. We had to do what scores of citizens were being obligated to do: Filing bankruptcy became our short-term and humiliating fix. Through lots of sacrifice, we paid off our debtors within two years, on our terms, even settling our balance with Dr. McCann for bringing into the world two lovable creatures.

The four-year-old Belrose Dance Studio was now beginning to slowly emerge as a budding presence, and it was clear that we desperately needed more room. We, with much apprehension, made the laborious decision to continue with our set-upon life and not settle for a government position.

So we made our third move into quite a frightful duplex that would make for a bigger studio (that was good), but was a very limited space for our family of four plus our mutt Nanette (that was bad). Davy was not yet three, and Dea not one. People still thought of David and Margie Belrose as 'kids'.

We painted out the hideousness of the building in and out, and it was all that. We fixed it up as artistically as possible within our limited means. Because we were on a busy thoroughfare, displaying a large sign in front of said building that read to the world "The Belrose Dance Studio" it prepared our school to quickly grow. After three winning years, we were eager for an even a larger studio and quarters to live in. We felt we had "almost arrived."

Here is another digression once again, sorry.

The beautiful and talented woman, Davida Wills Herwin, who suggested, encouraged, and insisted that my play and now this book be written, she would not take 'no' for an answer.

This energetic and adorable young girl began her dance training on a scholarship as an already talented nine-year-old, in this duplex. We inexplicably were able to make our new digs into a decent enough studio, but still with cramped living area. We taught her with joy, for years, and in turn, she babysat for our young family, came with us on a vacation, helped where she could, accomplishing countless unselfish and creative undertakings and magically performing in our many productions. Davida is a true friend to 'the me'. Scores of others were henceforth developed under her guidance and love also.

After training with us the time came for her to teach in our school during her brilliant college career. At one point, she formed her own innovative, but brief, dance company, because her plan was to set off for L.A. to a well-deserved and ingenious professional life.

For many creative years she has been teaching dancing, acting, directing, producing, at the prestigious school, Cross Roads, in Santa Monica.

Along with her teaching and directorial work, she began effectively to write plays and became a published writer of at least three books, as of 2010. She continues to pursue this artistic endeavor and is compelled to do so, with her generous god given gifts and talent.

Back to our stroll. Nope not yet.

Here is another digression...

David and I had been the dance teachers of three adopted and loved children of the same family for the previous seven years. They loyally followed us to our three separate locations. Dorothy and Sol Abrams. Our little family of four were invited to spend many beautiful holidays in their gorgeous Ross home. We swam in their pool and enjoyed the many healthy meals prepared by Dorothy. We were friends. "Consider our home your home always." One day, after their daughter, Gail's, ballet class, Dorothy spontaneously tossed out a remark: "If you ever want to invest money, Sol can help." Of course we had no money to invest in anything, not then or ever, damn. But upon hearing the word "invest", it tenaciously glued itself to my curious, quest-seeking mind.

Dorothy could not ever have imagined that her words would alter the lives of Margie, David, Davy and Dea Belrose in such a way that would never have occurred but for her casual remark. Thank you, thank you, Dorothy."

SCENE TWENTY-SIX

In February of 1962, David and Margie slowly took a studio-searching expedition, in the city we almost began to think of as our "hometown."

We found ourselves on Fifth Avenue, the very street Mr. Kahn suggested we should try to find a location for our school when we first decided to move to San Rafael. There stood a unique, small church that was obviously vacant, and it caught my inquisitive eye and imagination.

The Kahn family spent summer weekends here and were acquainted with this sleepy city and pretty tree lined streets. He also suggested we buy a Volkswagen (which we did eventually, twice).

"David, look at the old empty church, wouldn't it make a perfect place for our school and maybe even a theatre, all we would need and want?" David pooh-poohed the idea. "Maybe if we could find a warehouse that might work out to fit our needs; a theatre, school and living quarters, that just could be the answer, Margie."

He perused the newspaper and immediately followed up on an ad for a warehouse, quoting: "$219 a month", being the picky Virgo that he often was, "Why not $220? $219 is a bit odd." He called Mr. Steinert, the owner of a warehouse, and without ado was taken to scope it out. "Well, will it work?"

"It won't work, it is a real old warehouse. I guess that's why $219 a month." The next day Mr. Steinert called.

"Let me show you two kids (we were still kids then) the perfect place. You won't believe it."

He picked us up in his car and as he slowed down to park, out of my wide gaping mouth, and racing heart: "Mr. Steinert, you don't mean this sweet little vacant church?"

"Yes, it would be just so right for you two." When we cautiously walked in, it still had many pews, pulpit, and an altar. The Trinity Lutheran Church, of which Mr. Steinert was a parishioner, had just erected a much larger edifice of worship and was still in the throes of moving everything out of the very place we were now goggling at.

"David we've gone to heaven. After all, this has been a church. Look, look, look how big this room is, good grief, look here in the back is an apartment. David, the whole downstairs is as big as the upstairs, we can do so much with it. Just can't believe it, but how can we do it?"

We purposefully left the downstairs door unlocked. The same door that long ago became our apartment door in the rear of the theatre. In leaving that afternoon we knew it was important that we return and really look it over by ourselves. We called Sol with unleashed hope and excitement: "Sol, please come right over." He hesitated, as he was a criminal lawyer working on an important case: "Sol, this concerns the Belrose family, our very lives." Sensing this was very urgent; he immediately came over at nine p.m. We drove to the place that we felt with every fiber of our being was made to order for us.

In quietly creeping around with flashlight in hand, we three walked and talked non-stop through all the possibilities. It was absolutely and definitely right for us: "Look Sol, the peak ceiling is even high enough to build a stage and install theatrical lighting. Sol, this building belongs to the Belrose family and you have to help us."

"Let's have lunch tomorrow and we'll talk." Of course, there was no sleeping that night, dreaming while awake of the incredible potential. My heart was madly racing, thinking and fantasizing about so many incredible ideas for what could be our promising future.

We met for lunch and apprehensively sat there while tightly hugging our two little ones. Somehow the strength of courage was there for 'me' to suddenly blurt out: "Sol, as I pleaded last night, that building belongs to the Belrose family and you have to help."

"Well, if I have to help you, I guess I will."

"Where did the daring come from—the nerve?"

Our children were a delightful four and six years old, and our own still young lives were excitedly beaming ahead of us.

"It was meant to be, it had to be." We called Mr. Steinert too early the next morning, and a quick meeting was arranged with the powers that be. We almost ran to the bank as fast as we could with Sol slowly tagging behind, before anything could topple our dreams. Sol generously put up the down payment, which we, by sacrifice and many miracles, paid off in two years. We could see our benefactor was clearly relieved that we could settle the enormous debt in such a short time. We were thankful too but I don't know how we did it.

"Oh yes I do: scrambled eggs, tuna fish, hot dogs, beef stew, meat loaf, spaghetti, beans, second hand clothes and shoes, no movies, no vacations, no outings. Frugality was the thrust, and that's how it was accomplished."

A lot of hoops had to be jumped through forward and backward, side ways, plus a back flip or two, with the planning department, the building inspector, the licensing department, the fire department, the city planner, and even the city attorney. "Gloriously, it went on and on." (Bare in mind, we had never owned any real estate, and had no concept of all the intricacies).

But in spite of the endless areas and paper work that had to be ferreted out, we DID IT. David performed a thoroughly Virgo-genius-organized plan that was admired by all concerned.

He methodically and vigorously arranged all the information and permits together and within two days, presented his intelligent outline to the decision makers.

"Oh, how he would have loved this age of computers. He could quite easily have become addicted to the technology of today. Very unlike 'me'.

At ten a.m. on a promising sunny Sunday, July fourth, 1962, it became our true independence day. The Belrose family took ownership of a special kind of building that sits on the piece of land designated as 1415 Fifth Ave. It would, quick as a wink, become the Belrose theatre, school and home.

During this gigantic transition, Dorothy insisted on taking care of Dea in their home for several weeks to allow us the time to accomplish all that was begging to get done.

However the incongruity is that I could only collapse in a trance like catatonic state the first week, with the scary trepidation of what we had done. With the unforgiving fear that perhaps we would not be able to meet our financial and creative obligations, I simply could not move, could not eat or sleep, could not take care of my family. David did not know what to do with me but patiently wait, as he brought me food.

Sol walked in with Dea holding his hand. He waited a week, not really knowing what to expect as I just sat unable to move, and he impatiently ordered: "Margie stand up right now and do what you allegedly said you could and would do."

Taking a humongous sigh of relief, I did just that.

In our studio's first seven years, in three locations, we were simply a dance studio and never stopped loving it, but now with our very own 1913 historical building, it afforded us bigger artistic and creative dreams. We re-named it:

"The Belrose Studio Theatre"

Before we knew it, we had evolved into a theatrical school of teaching dance, acting, singing and producing many shows, for all ages, through the subsequent years.

Davida was by our side through it all, with ideas, encouragement, help and love.

2010 marked forty-eight years, living and doing business in our own treasured possession, smack-dab in the middle of town, in a building specified as 1415 Fifth Avenue, San Rafael.

This was, in truth, a "show biz" story.

We two innocents were at the right place at the right time, knew the right people, and had the ability, tenacity, courage, talent, and just plain guts to do whatever would be required for our dream to come to full realization."

WHAT A GIFT FROM THE GODS. That have never stopped looking after 'the me' and mine.

Of course we remained close to the Abrams family for many years. We continued to visit them, still sharing special days, swimming in their pool, barbecuing. Still teaching their three not yet fully grown youngsters.

Quite some years later, a message was delivered to 'me' that our kind friend and generous, benefactor, Sol Abrams, was very ill. With not a moment to spare, I quickly sped over to the beautiful home we had shared so many joyful times in, not yet knowing what to expect. Sol was slumped over in a chair, so very frail. While kneeling down to hold him we cried together as our tears mingled. Looking up into his face that had many stories to tell, he hugged me with a surge of strength that he was probably surprised he still had:

"Dear Margie, you have done everything you ever said you would. I cannot forget your urgent pleas for my help. How did you become such an honest and good person with your sad and parentless background? I love you and your family. If I had to do it all over again for you, I would. Do you think I am about to see David?"

"Yes you will, Sol, and very soon. You will also set eyes on other people that shared love and friendship with you. Thank you Sol, for everything, for giving 'me', an unloved and abused orphan, and my very much-loved family, a life we could never have had without your trusting belief, love and generous help. Goodbye for now my dear friend, and we'll meet again too." Within a few months, he indeed went to join David and others in a sphere we mortals know nothing of, yet.

At this juncture David had just recently passed away. I will write of this in the next scene.

I AM GRATEFUL
LYRICS BY MARGIE BELROSE
Dedicated to
Sol and Dorothy Abrams

I AM GRATEFUL FOR ALMOST EVERYTHING
THOUGH THAT DOESN'T SEEM A POSSIBILITY
THE TREES ACHING TO REACH THE SKY
THE BIRDS THAT FLY INCREDIBLY HIGH
THE LITTLE BABIES THAT CRY AND CRY
THE SWEETNESS OF EACH DAY GONE BY
THE ABILITY WE ALL HAVE TO SURVIVE
I AM GRATEFUL FOR MY HOME,
EVEN WHEN LEFT ALONE
I THEN LOOK AT MY BOOKS AND PICTURES
AND I AM NOT ALONE.
MY TREASURES ARE SO MUCH A PART OF MY HOME
AND LISTENING TO MUSIC
OH, HOW IT ALL INSPIRES MY CREATIVE JUICES
HOW COULD I POSSIBLY BE ALONE
WHAT A WORLD WE HAVE TO BE SO GRATEFUL FOR
IF THEY'RE JUST WERE NO WARS
THEN THE HARMONY WE ALL LONG FOR
WOULD START EACH DAY WITH A SONG
FULL OF JOY AND THEN
WHAT MORE COULD WE ASK FOR
WHAT MORE COULD WE BE GRATEFUL FOR

© 2009 Margie Belrose

SCENE TWENTY-SEVEN

Unfortunately, David could not share all the heady, exciting and creative years; the years that were still waiting to shine on us in this prized building he loved and worked diligently to acquire for his beloved family and our future.

The acquisition of this special structure up to that point in David's life could possibly have been his crowning glory.

On an early foggy morning, October fifteen, 1971, my husband had a massive heart attack. No earlier signs of this alarming tragedy were evident. He had just enjoyed his forty-sixth year on September fifteenth, one month earlier. Davy was fifteen, Dea thirteen, and Margie was much too young to be a widow.

We lived a marriage of eighteen years together, but he spent only nine in this wondrous place that fulfilled our unique dreams when he travelled, with foreboding, to meet up with his loving maker. He affected hundreds of lives in his short, ingenious and gentle lifetime. Mr. David's quiet influence is still felt to this day, not only by the three of us, but by more people than can be enumerated in the next decade.

To speak of David's death…

"Oh, I do abhor that foreboding word: It is so final with no opportunity of making up, no stolen moments of reconciling differences, no chance of another night of considerate and tender loving, no time to make faltering plans that could and would change daily, no chance of anything at all.

It was to be only the arduous and burdensome knowledge that the sun might never shine on 'me' and my children again.

We would only know the bleakness of each cold, absolutely black night- only feel the complete loneliness and baffling bewilderment of each day that would surely come with sorrow.

I realized the possibility that my world, as had been known for so many civilized years, might never be warm and secure again, to tenderly engulf 'the me' and my loved ones with safety and love.

It was all so unkind, unexpected and abrupt, so terribly, terribly remorseless. It would carry such a blue sadness never to be experienced again by 'the me', my family and for many people. To selfishly put it: "What happens to the forlorn Margie and my fatherless children now? How can the massive amount of epic problems be solved exclusively by myself, one person- troubles that need the smarts of two people to solve?"

These were the disturbing and heartbreaking thoughts running at break neck speed through my muddled and misty mind. With concerted valor, my taut body sat upright in the uncomfortable pew of the next-door mortuary. The funeral parlor was overflowing with several hundred mourners.

Sobs were noiselessly striving to come out of this hundred-and-five-pound individual, while I was simultaneously trying to console my two panicky, bewildered young ones. I had to gently instill in them their own hidden strengths. They were too young to comprehend the gravelly road ahead, but would only too soon be forced to summon up their yet to be found courage.

"This was to be a frantic, unbearable point in time. Somehow I had to find my own inner strength and bravery that had never been touched upon in the same way. It was now rushing forth with no thought of kindness, to vanish from my soul with each burning tear."

Whatever it was about David's demeanor and obvious inner strength, no one even thought or attempted to get in his face. But now: "Who was to protect 'me' and mine from a world of uncertainty that was quickly crowding in with hardly a care or compassion?" As a grown woman this was my most defenseless place. Feeling weak, my "alone" was beyond any clever words of description.

The childhood memories of abandonment I lived through and the endless disconcerting emotions came surging back to again haunt 'me'. A superhuman effort had been established in 'me' for years to not look back too often, and to bury forever, those long ago terrorizing emotions.

In those years there also was helplessness and many things seemed frightening and completely futile.

To find an expression, even today, more than half a century later, to express to you of a time in my life that felt more than pitch black, is not possible. This now was to be a time in my shaky existence of continuous changes, confusion, and the familiar deep-seated terror. This was a time when "not so good people" ruthlessly barged in and exited out of my sad life with their hidden agendas, and more often than not, with motives just this side of selfish evil.

The seemingly 'good' people would eventually show their true colors that might even be called 'foul' and were possibly intended to foster hurt on 'me' and mine.

The unexpected abandonment of David's leaving his family was hardly a new experience.

Had he taken care of himself, and let 'me' help him, had he talked to 'me' about his own deep sorrows, he might still be in this beautiful building he loved. He would then observe his children mature into exceptional, talented, and kind adults.

David could have warmly watched with such pride and relished in the beauty and goodness of a lovely granddaughter, Rachel.

He affectionately would have seen the changes in this building he treasured, in this seamless and ever-evolving theatre company and school. He might have taken pride in my personal growth that we surely would have shared with happiness, but still with friendly controversy. Maybe not, perhaps. That would never have changed but would invariably be packed with conjecture and fulfillment. David might have tripped over himself with noble pride and joy.

He was a writer and understood the English language so well and better than most. "Don't know if Margie B. would have dared to venture into his personal creative dominion with my play, this book, and the lyrics that unexpectedly spilled out of 'me'

Along the way, somehow, David became a gifted professional photographer and to learn from him was inspiring and took a step beyond exciting. My new part-time aspiration was to become somewhat of a photographer, much like he became. "Was he ever threatened by this new inquisitive exploration of mine? Don't know. What did he think when the 'me' registered for classes in photography at the local community college, and subsequently installed my own dark room?"

He never said, and it never occurred to 'me' to question, nor even thought about it at the time, only now in long belated retrospect.

"Had I not been an obsessively goal-driven dancer and teacher, quite possibly a photographer of human faces and bodies would have been my chosen creative career."

The last day of a life that he all too soon came to despair, he seemed unusually calm, peaceful, almost resigned to something that I just could not put my finger on at the time.

"Maybe he knew he had to make his exodus, that he could do nothing more, could contribute nothing more, in the spiraling world, of his brief life." But he could have, he could have. He simply gave up. "Oh, David, why did you give up? I miss you with all my heart, as do your adoring children. Damn, damn, damn."

On that day of a gray and foggy October fourteenth afternoon when, with much effort, he pulled his emotionally broken and disillusioned self out of a bed he no longer cared to share with 'me'. Although there were times he was invited into 'my' loveless bed. For several tenuous moments we would tenderly share caresses with unspoken longing. Then, with undeclared sorrow and love, he would slip back to his own lonely, empty and sorrowful place of retreat, of protection.

On that same day, about three p.m., he dressed and slowly walked across the studio floor, "Could we go to lunch?" This had not happened for almost two years. With a happy and unexpected coincidence, at the same time my dear and generous friend, Davida, walked into the theatre: "Would you finish my afternoon classes? David needs me."

We walked out our theatre door, with our hands entwined in the unusual and tender way that began when we first loved one another. The unspoken promise was to have an afternoon repast and talk, at his favorite restaurant (the same restaurant Sol and the Belrose family made our life changing agreement).

"Margie, I am going to make so many new promises that will amend everything starting right now today. I am so sorry for so much. Please put your, our, wedding ring on again? I miss you my Margie." The wedding ring he spoke of had angrily flown off my finger several years before. It happened on a day when David was particularly unkind and sarcastic in his biting words and treatment of 'me'. 'The 'me' that no longer felt married or loved. The 'me' that didn't even want to be and sought a means to escape from far away. The unbearable hurt was so vast I didn't want to look at him ever again.

Sometimes I just wanted to disappear, to dissolve or throw myself out a window. But with my two young and caring children to continue raising and love, it was not conceivable.

When we returned a few hours later, he sat down to begin gathering many colored pens and paper. He needed to spread it all out and organize a multicolored schedule. It was a habit he was compelled to exercise and always did when he wanted to make "Oh so many changes and renew promises. When he felt inspired and things might be achievable."

LIVE IN THE MOMENT

Lyrics by Margie Belrose

Dedicated to David Belrose

LIVE IN THE MOMENT FOR THAT'S ALL WE HAVE

SMALL BEGINNINGS CAN LEAD

TO BIGGER AND BETTER THINGS

THINGS THAT MAKE US GLAD – SOMETIMES SAD

BUT IF WE DON'T LIVE IN THE MOMENT

EACH AND EVERY DAY

AND ESPECIALLY IF WE FORGET TO PRAY

GIVING THANKS FOR EVEN THE LITTLE THINGS

THEN THE PRECIOUS MOMENTS OF EVERY DAY

ARE LOST TO US IN EVERY WAY

FOR THAT'S ALL WE HAVE AFTER ALL THERE IS

REALLY NOTHING MORE

Our thirteen year-old snip of a tomboy was snuggled in her loving daddy's lap, giving him gentle kisses on his eyelids, on an evening that would all too soon serve up unimaginable sorrow for the three of us. The night of October fourteen, 1971 held countless unspoken promises that would never come to be enjoyed.

That adorable tomboy brushed his hair, cut his nails, rubbed his feet, massaged his shoulders, and kissed the tips of his fingers, as they hardly watched "The Dirty Dozen." I took my tired self to bed in another room since it was necessary to get up too early for my job at the middle school where my three hours of morning time was filled with teaching jazz dancing.

Very early the following morning of October fifteenth, young Dea came running out of breath and crying to wake Davy and 'me:' "Daddy is making all kinds of scary noises. He must be having a nightmare, come and help him, hurry." And we thought he WAS having a nightmare. The ambulance arrived within a few anxiety filled minutes, but David had already, maybe with reluctance, traveled to another unidentified sphere.

In a peculiar way, perhaps he planned his departure, not to hurt anyone, but just to quietly leave so HE wouldn't suffer any more, It could be, he believed, that there no longer was any strength left in him to continue the exhausting fight, and could not in his physical and mental excruciating pain.

These were things no one knew anything of then. I am compelled to question them now in my silent and endless search for answers.

In my scrambled thinking of so many of my David's habits, an unexpected awareness came to me recently. "I don't believe I ever saw tears in David's eyes in all our up and down years together."

He apparently was unable to share his torments only his crushing and angry verbal tirades. But not the perceived disappointments in himself, the regrets about his father, the stepmother that didn't want or love him, and the loss of a mother he never knew, but so often needed to. This is all just an educated conjecture on my part. He was very much a man unto himself, with many multifaceted good and bad behaviors.

"I miss hearing his unusual, marvelous, resonant voice, miss his teaching 'me', our daily talks that we both took time out and eagerly looked forward to, miss dancing with him, miss seeing him walk with such grace, miss seeing him shave, miss seeing him sit and just think, miss seeing him with the children he adored – playing chess, Risk, scrabble and other word games. He "let" them win some of the time, or so he thought."

I am filled with a great deal of contentment to have been Mrs. David John Belrose for eighteen years. The good years cannot be, nor should be, denied, but there were some very dire years we wrestled through that cannot be dismissed either. It has been the major plus in my life, to be the mother of his children, our children.

The people who knew and loved him as "Mr. David," miss him too, that's a certainty.

A DAY HAS NEVER GONE BY

Lyrics & Music by Margie Belrose
Arranger, Gillian Lovejoy
Dedicated to the loving memory of David Belrose
or "Mr. David"

A DAY HAS NEVER GONE BY
THAT I DON'T THINK OF YOU
YOUR SMILE – YOUR LAUGH – YOUR TOUCH
YOUR SWEETNESS THROUGH AND THROUGH
THE TIME HAS LINGERED ON
THE DAYS HAVE BEEN LONG
AND THE NIGHTS EVEN MORE
BUT I JUST CAN'T FORGET
NO MATTER HOW I TRY
YOUR SMILE- YOUR LAUGH – YOUR TOUCH
YOUR SWEETNESS THROUGH AND THROUGH
BUT WE ALL GO ON AND THAT WE MUST DO
BUT NO MATTER WHAT HAPPENS
I SHALL ALWAYS THINK OF
YOUR SMILE – YOUR LAUGH – YOUR TOUCH
YOUR SWEETNESS THROUGH AND THROUGH
I SHALL ALWAYS ALWAYS THINK OF YOU
I SUPPOSE I STILL LOVE YOU TOO – EVEN NOW

SCENE TWENTY-EIGHT

Before David made his necessary, but surely his dreaded, farewell to a world he had begun to feel so alienated from, he had become an inspiration to innumerable people: He was, in my mind, a renaissance man of sorts: David was an exceptional director. Many people learned a great deal from him, 'me' especially. He was my teacher, was an actor, a ballroom dancer/teacher, an innovative choreographer, a photographer with an artistic knowledge of lighting and composition and he carried that exceptional talent into our theatre when stage lighting was installed.

David John Belrose was a playwright with scores of original plays to his credit, all written for various ages of students and others. He had an unusual sense of humor; he was fun. He was a productive band manager.

There is no doubt Mr. David's students admired the way he directed. He taught and treated everyone with fairness, patience, affection, and respect, never playing favorites. He was a guru and teacher of life to many and certainly to 'the me', but paradoxically, not to himself.

He was somewhat of a psychologist, and could have been. He and I both prevented the intended suicides of two students, plus going to the legal aid of two teenage boys avoiding serious jail time. He certainly was a philosopher. He was a thinker and would have relished being part of a creative "think tank."

The most fulfilling professional thing for 'king' David was that he had developed into an exceptional and sensitive lyricist while working with his long-time composer partner and indeed his friend, Don Deane. He loved words, consequently wrote many songs, but the song that was recorded by the King Sisters, and was performed in one of their Easter TV shows, was described on the album cover as a "lovely tone poem."

WHO WOULD REMEMBER
Lyrics by David Belrose Music by Don Deane
Dedicated to Sue Sue Finegan, Davy and Dea Belrose

WHO WOULD REMEMBER MERRY-GO-ROUNDS

PINK COTTON CANDY CARNIVAL SOUNDS

HOW HIGH DID SWINGS GO

HOW FAST DID TRAINS

HOW SOFT WAS SNOWING HOW WET WAS THE RAIN

JACK-FROSTED WINTERS

BAREFOOTED SPRINGS

WHO WOULD REMEMBER ALL OF THOSE THINGS

WHO WOULD REMEMBER

NAMES ETCHED IN SAND

DADDY LOVES MARY

MY DADDY'S HAND

NO ONE BUT ME

NO ONE BUT ME

The most endearing qualities of the brilliant but short-lived David Belrose was his unabashed love for our two children, this distinctive and precious building, and maybe 'me' too. While he was productively managing two easy rock bands, exciting plans were in the making for him to trek off to L.A. each Monday (to return home on the weekends) and establish himself as an "A&R man" for Beachwood Music Publishing.

On that exhilarating Monday morning when he was to board an early plane of creative adventure to L.A., he simply wasn't able to emotionally. David could tell you, without a doubt, exactly HOW to do it, but found it beyond his own inner strength to do it. "Was he afraid of success and consequently sabotaged himself? I don't know, though so many of his life patterns would suggest it."

In 1968, three years before his demise (that is an awful word too), he went on a victorious diet and was able to shed 68 pounds in one year. He again became the slender, healthy, handsome man he was when we joined our love together. He was writing profusely, was very productive and exuded happiness every day and unselfishly spread it around.

We were ALL happy. He was about to conquer the world of music and himself. Our family was abounding with anticipation, and optimistic of our futures.

Then one day, with no warning or obvious reason, he lost all motivation, his personality changed, and he began to put the weight back on. He then started to do something he had never done before: David began to drink, and smoke more than ever. My lost husband was helplessly descending on a self-destructive course.

He crawled into his own protective bed for the better part of two years. The only time he ventured out of his defensive cradle was to coach Davy in his track pursuits several times a week. A sport he knew very well, as he himself had been on a high school track team. The man I knew as my cheerful husband was more often than not very depressed.

This serious state of affairs was not recognized by anyone. At that time in 1971 maybe depression wasn't to be taken seriously, maybe the depressed person was just thought to be lazy, maybe the person was sick? I don't know the answers. If this had been realized, perhaps, only perhaps, he might have found professional help.

After his sudden departure, and when I finally took the neglected but now required time to search through his belongings, there stood among the disarray of his belongings, an old, slightly battered stand up trunk. This old fashion trunk whispered to 'me', "Hey, look in me." I opened the urging of the trunk and it shocked 'me' to set my eyes on many dozens of empty bottles of Excedrin and Valium.

It can only be surmised he must have been in an enormous amount of pain, physically and mentally. He hid all this from his loving family and again possibly, only possibly, there might have been some help had he shared his pain with someone. But, don't think he would have permitted such help, even with his extensive background in psychology.

He was his own private person. He sought to live like an island unto himself and urged 'me' to follow suit, but 'me' could not, to his consternation. This might have been one of my failings in our ambiguous relationship, don't know that either. I strongly suspect the Valium, which I didn't know he was ingesting for years, had an unforeseeable and resultant detrimental affect on his personality and mood.

Valium is a sinister drug. Oh, this is just my take, but I believe it to be true after investigating the side effects. However, on the other side of the dark coin, I also found hundreds of funny, touching, tender, poignant, clever, lyric lines, scribbled on odd pieces of paper anywhere and everywhere and they touched on the essence of the

HEART AND TALENT OF THE TRUE AND PURE
DAVID BELROSE

Don't get 'me' wrong; David Belrose had a dark side that he displayed only to his insecure Margie. He could be ruthlessly sarcastic, could rationalize anything to his favor, and was capable of deliberately throwing mean, hurtful and hateful diatribes at 'me'.

So often he would and did invalidate a troubled 'me' in a snap. David was, in his quite and subtle way, selfishly controlling. My husband was skillful at pushing my buttons. I tried to fight back, but was simply not clever or strong enough.

He would walk away after the torrential pouring out of an unforgiving harangue, leaving 'me' in a puddle of stinging tears that would not stop dripping off the end of my wet nose for countless hours. Then, I was left to cope with my unending depression alone, causing a continuous stream of suicidal thoughts that took many months to subside. No one was the wiser of my silent anguish.

This long ago emotionally damaged, Margie Leonides/ Belrose, alone bore the burden of his deep unexplained anger and disappointments. He was helpless to escape his own tortured memories that I knew nothing of, and therefore he so often proved; "hurt people, hurt people" Possibly approximating my forever hurt, oh so hurt, sister.

A small digression again, please
At this juncture of my story
It does seem a lot of words have been devoted:

- To the heartless father I barely knew but would somehow forever fear.

- To my desperately unhappy, bitter and oh so unbelievably complex sister.

- To my life of punishment in the two orphanages, especially St. Vincent's, and the vicious Sister Mary Matthew.

- To my first, endeared, and kind friend, lovely Sister Theresa.

- To the forever merciless callous birth mother that never was.

- To my dear Thea who loved 'me'.

- To David who was enamored by 'me', but was difficult to be happy with so often. And what ultimately held us together was our love, our children and our theatre.

- Also to the giving Kahns, my teachers, my friends.

- To the generosity of Sol and Dorothy Abrams that changed the lives of the Belrose family. But for them this life I have been living, with my family, in this priceless building, that is so distinguishing, would not be.

- To my more than three years at Lodi High, and the friends there.

- To the Ferrones who saved 'me', just in the nick time, and were so much a part of the 'me' for years. They truly changed my life. They became my life.

"How could I not?

All these people and circumstances were the various batches of tenacious glue that kept the near destructive possibility of my life from crumbling into dust and nothingness.

SCENE TWENTY-NINE

Because of my young children's honest efforts to be happy and productive despite David's unexpected journey from this planet, they both successfully graduated from high school. Davy went to the local junior college, for two years, all the while working, performing, playing and teaching his drums.

Dea graduated as a junior, performing, playing the piano, dancing and then running off to U.C.L.A. at a young seventeen years old on a partial scholarship she cleverly applied for by herself with the help of a counselor.

While in L.A., Dea auditioned for and was chosen to perform on the then-popular Gong Show, winning it.

Shortly after, she was accepted into the long standing and nationally famed American Folk Ballet, a perfect company for her five foot two body,

They artistically used and further developed her exceptional talents in tap and jazz to her very best ability, while performing most every day for them.

Then one unexpected and unforeseen day, the company's CEDA funds were suddenly withdrawn, by order of our president, and they had to close down after many creative years in existence.

It was Davy's idea to start the costume shop, calling it "The Belrose Onstage Backstage Shop", in a Victorian house (several blocks from 'me').

Davy really wanted a department store for the theatre. San Rafael wasn't ready for such an ambitious dream in 1978 and probably never will be, believe it to be too highly specialized.

We had to put one of those hateful mortgages on my building to purchase his house so he could live in it and conduct his new business.

After several years it was doing pretty well, 'the me' thought, but not up to his expectations. One day in an unusual negative mood: "Mom the shop just isn't my cup of tea, please take it over." We had to sacrifice his charming house at a great financial beating, even though he was able to sell it. Then our only alternative was to move the shop to the lower level of the theatre. "Oh, God, what to do with a costume shop?"

This person you are reading about is a dancer and a teacher. But in time, the shop flourished; not in the original design it was conceived, but the changes eventually turned out to be wise and they continue to be (oh sure a few bumps here and there).

My ambitious son David wanted instead to own a comedy club he named "The Flatiron" (the shape of the building) in 1980. He knew many of the comedians so he naturally had faith it would succeed, even though he was an inexperienced but eager twenty-four year-old. We were not wise enough and we both failed to investigate the comedy business: "What to do, what not to do? Does anyone really know how to successfully run a club? By the hundreds they go down the tubes all over the country. We didn't know that then."

We were happily skipping along on Davy's exciting hot emotions plus his boundless enthusiasm. Actually, it did well for a couple of years but had two main problems. First one being his partner (who I begged him not to partner up with). He was incompatible in any number of ways, and also, the fact that only beer, wine and popcorn were served. No menu, no liquor. The problems were ignorantly and innocently unforeseeable, even though they gobbled us up in our inexperienced faces and we didn't recognize the upcoming events that crashed ahead so quickly.

The problems glaringly blinked at us with flashing red lights we didn't notice until too late. It was inevitable Davy's dream was bound to fail with the fickle public, when the rare novelty of a full-time comedy club wore off in San Rafael. It was financially devastating for the Belrose family. My son had the determined dream that his club would be an all-time financial lifesaver for our family.

By this time, I had to put two more mortgages on my dear building in a brave effort to save Davy's club. But it was not enough. The club, with hundreds of terror-filled emotions, folded and Davy had to file a mortifying bankruptcy. "Oh, God, I owe my own mortgage plus two more very big ones. How can they be paid every month, and what can be done to help my young man through his months of depression that would inescapably follow?"

I dejectedly sat myself down in a daze, to write a short list of possible financial solutions that might work out with my school, the productions and the costume shop. It was an unbearably convoluted and near to impossible situation to resolve: "It all made 'me' just want to escape and hide away in bed for the rest of my life."

Dread and the cold sweats overflowed every cell of my thin body every minute of every fear-filled day and night. This was followed by abruptly waking up in a panic from horrific nightmares, to hot tears that soaked my pillow and hair.

In 1962 we bought our historical building for just $55,000 including all the equipment, building the stage, lights, light board, chairs, curtains, fire escape, sheet rocking the lower lever, etc. At that time it was a great deal of money. Of course the mortgage was settled several times over through the years and refinanced, and in fact, can't remember how many times.

"Putting three major mortgages on this building to rescue it, and 'the me', was not enough. The payments with no compassion, greedily stared at the troubled 'me' the first of every frightful month. There was no let-up, and the demands became impossible to meet. Something more than mammoth had to be achieved."

It was urgent to quickly figure out what could be done to pay off an impossible obligation of over $200,000, not including my own mortgage. This insane debt could only be described as "insurmountably austere. The short list of what can liberate us, after receiving a foreboding foreclosure notice one terrifying rainy day, included cleaning houses, waitressing, and deciding what hours might conceivably work out with my school's still busy schedule."

An incredible backbreaking, six-year plan was hastily hammered out while trying to hold back irrepressible tears that would not stop. The plan of action was to clean houses and offices from seven a.m. to nine p.m. I had to quickly tramp back to the theatre at two p.m. to teach a few young classes, then off to service offices at seven p.m.

Some days found 'me' cleaning twenty seven toilets while singing with all the daring in me: "Pack Up Your Troubles come on Get Happy and Flush all Your Cares away."

One night while scurrying about doing my waitressing job, Beth Ashley a friend and well known and beloved writer walked in for a late dinner. I wanted to hide, but I had to face the music. "Margie what are you doing here?" "I'm in trouble, Beth and I'm saving my ass." she was sad and consequently wrote two columns about my dilemma and we have remained friends.

"Thank you Ken Vix, my life long friend, for hiring 'me' to be a cocktail waitress at your successful bar."

To mention something of Ken Vix: in the early years of our school, he taught and developed an exciting twirling majorette team of pretty girls that performed with Ken while he flipped his own baton as the drum major. Then I think he had to go in the service. Afterwards, when he could get time off between things, he performed in many of our shows. "Those were good times. Ken."

On weekends, I worked as a banquet waitress at a local country club that became a portion of my saving grace. I also had to do our shows on Friday and Saturday nights. "Now how all this rehearsing and performing was accomplished is still a mystery, beyond description and nothing short of a blessed miracle, even to 'me'. There must have been an angel on my gentle shoulders. Otherwise how could it be, or maybe my bed never welcomed 'me'. Without the help of Davy and Dea's personal sacrifices, the marvel of all marvels, would not have occurred, we would have lost our treasure. Where did the time and energy come from? Don't know. Had to dovetail all the pressing obligations somehow. In time the impossible effort was somehow completed for this tired and grateful person and my family."

Before this incomprehensible situation, Dea quickly left Los Angeles and her New York dreams to rush home as fast as her little Honda would allow. She unselfishly helped clean the eight houses a week, took two other jobs, besides teaching and performing. Davy worked as a bartender and did his share of cleaning some of the banks most nights before his bartending job, while now living back in the theatre.

That hard-to-grasp and turbulent period of time, for Davy, Dea, and 'the me', will always be remembered as the "terrible eighties." The unbelievable became believable, in that all the mortgages, except my own one, were dissolved and we three, because of working harmoniously together, were somewhat set free of the heavy financial burden of over $200,000.

"In 1982 it was like climbing the highest mountain peak or swimming the Golden Gate daily from Alcatraz, most likely doing both."

Being unable to physically take care of this special historical building during those six nightmarish years, a lot of work had to be done to make it appear pretty again and cared for.

Fortunately, in 1981, time was somehow carved out to legally turn the Belrose into a 501-c-3 non-profit California organization. In so doing, it paved the way for The Belrose to get community service volunteers to contribute their talents and physical help. Thus we were also able to ease a tax burden off our shaky financial backs.

Our non-profit status has been a Godsend and continues to be. During that same period of time we were advised to apply for a beer and wine license for our dinner shows, which it, too, has been financially a gigantic plus in helping the Belrose to remain financially solvent.

Even with so much volunteer help, another small mortgage had to be taken out on the building for a variety of repairs, but this time it was a manageable solution.

The building, the school, the costume shop, my humble digs and theatre have gone through an evolution of never-ending, but creative changes. Some clever ones, some foolish ones, and some ill conceived ones. "I wish it could be said that I had the foresight and there had been a master plan originally, but so what, the important thing is that progress has been made and will continue. That's a given."

The year 2010 made the Belrose Theatrical School fifty-six years old, the theatre forty-eight, the costume shop thirty-three and 'the me'- well, who cares?

Every day my heart gently, but oh ever-so-powerfully, nudges 'me' in assurance: "You've been here since 1954. You're not an orphan, certainly not a crazy one (well, that one's up for grabs). Margie you have solid roots, you have a hometown to call your own, a loving family, a unique home, three small businesses that merge one to the other, and hundreds of true and helpful friends that have come to your aid when needed or asked. For someone with your background, Margie, this should not be, but here you are."

A Lucky Duck. Quack, quack, quack.

I LOVE THIS PLACE, IT'S BEEN MY HOME

Lyrics by Margie Belrose
I dedicate this song to this building
that has become an actual living thing

I LOVE THIS PLACE, IT'S BEEN MY HOME

I COULD NEVER EVER ROAM

MY KIDS GREW UP HERE, I NEVER HAD TO FEAR

IT WAS SAFE AND SO DEAR AND IT HAS BEEN

WHAT WE ALL LOVED AND HELD CLOSE

TOP TO BOTTOM, INSIDE AND OUT

NO ONE SAW IT ANOTHER WAY

IT'S BEEN OURS DAY AFTER DAY AFTER DAY

YOU SEE, IT'S BEEN MY HOME,

A PLACE WHERE I COULD NEVER ROAM

MY KIDS GREW UP HERE,

WE NEVER HAD TO FEAR

OH, YES, I'VE BEEN STUPID HERE AND THERE

AND THEY HAVE BEEN TOO

AS MUCH AS I'VE LOOKED AROUND

I GOTTA SAY

I LOVE THIS PLACE AND MY KIDS I HOLD DEAR

AND THAT'S THE SUM OF IT ALL

THAT'S THE SUM OF IT ALL. SO THERE

© 2009 Margie Belrose

SCENE THIRTY

To remember the years of the terrible eighties, even slightly, is too heartbreaking for my family to talk or think about. But nevertheless, in time, I sat my exhausted bum down with paper and pencil in a trembling right hand, one grateful morning as the sun was streaming thru a window warming my aching back. With unsuspecting glad tears streaming down my worn face by this time, and there was such powerful relief that took over every cell of my being with a sadness that was more than sad but was, slowly and gratefully, dissipating.

A compulsion came over me to write (in my scribbly fashion) of my sorrows and about the unbelievable fright and hurt of those petrifying times. I found myself traipsing as far back as my early neglected and abused years, and of David's unexpected death. I was surrounded in a grief-stricken emotion "It has been impossible to separate one era of my life from the other." How could it not? The first few written words on the paper nearly jumped out at 'me', "Margie these words might just be lyrics to a song" What would David have thought?"

I asked a songwriter friend to put down music to my first effort of a questionable and feeble attempt at lyrics. I had no idea this process was in 'me', but here they are. "Where did the idea come from, where did the words come from? I don't know."

STEP ASIDE

Lyrics by Margie Belrose
Music by Kayla Gold
I dedicate this song to the terrible Eighties
that we three Belroses escaped from

STEP ASIDE WHEN THE HURT COMES YOUR WAY

STEP ASIDE NO MATTER WHAT THEY DO OR SAY

WHEN THE TEARS COME, LET THEM FLOW

FOR ONLY YOU CAN KNOW THE PATHWAY TO YOUR SOUL

LET IT GO WHEN THE HURT COMES YOUR WAY

EVEN THOUGH YOU THINK YOU'VE LOST YOUR WAY

WHEN DISAPPOINTMENT HAUNTS YOUR EVERY MOVE

LET IT GO AND YOU'LL KNOW WHAT IS TRUE

THEN YOU CAN PULL YOUR LIFE TOGETHER

KEEP CHANGING LIKE THE WEATHER

BRUSH IT OFF AND LET IT RIDE

YOU CAN MAKE IT EVEN IF YOU HAVE TO FAKE IT

STEP ASIDE, STEP ASIDE

WHEN THE TEARS COME LET THEM FALL

FOR ONLY YOU CAN KNOW THE PATHWAY TO YOUR STAR

STEP ASIDE, JUST STEP ASIDE

AND YOU'LL KNOW WHO YOU REALLY ARE

SCENE THIRTY-ONE

It is now time for 'me' to again write or quite possibly reiterate about various other occurrences in both my unhappy and equally happy life that have made a difference.

Some mentions may even appear jumbled to you, as they sure do to 'me', the good and bad of it all. Some remembrances might turn out to be redundant, sorry about that. "Did you ever hear 'me' say I was a writer? Nope."

Forgive 'me', as there is a sick compulsion to reflect again about a father I barely knew. I have read: "We all need to know and respect our fathers: they form so much of our lives."

But for 'me' sadly NOT. Who and what was he really?

There are so many questions that cannot possibly be answered. Someone came to my door one morning, to inform 'me' he passed away in 1968, on his island of Samos, Greece when he was 68 years old, of his alcoholism. "Who are these 'someone's?'"

Someone (who?) also informed 'me' a very long time ago: "Sophie died on Christmas Eve years ago." I think the message was of Alzheimer's. I have asked myself, "What were her last lucid memories? Did she bother to remember or think of Margarete and Ethel, her unwanted and cast off children, in her coherent moments? Do I care? How terribly sad if I don't."

As said before, "How does the grapevine work?"

I have been in touch with a second cousin for the first time this year, 2010, to further research my convoluted life.

Mike and his family in Orlando, Florida, plus a first cousin, my father's brother's son, (got it?).

He is a spiritual, loving and generous man and a kind-hearted human being. John Leonides could have learned so much from this old soul, his nephew.

Second cousin Mike tried to answer some of my questions. He perused the only readable pamphlet in my possession, of my father's. Most of it is printed in beautiful Greek. In it, this man writes about studying in a seminary in Samos, to be ordained as a Greek Orthodox priest. However, there is no such holy institution there, according to Mike's interpretation.

In my father's family, for endless generations, almost all males were Greek Orthodox priests or monks. This included his own father, several brothers, grandfather and years of other male relatives. So, in my bemused judgment, he surely was educated, talented and with the intelligence to perform mass and other sacraments and ceremonies, and no one, even a perceptive person, would ever be the wiser.

In Mike's eagerness to further read the old worn-out document, it seems there were years Papa wrote about where he was, except in the years he mentions he was actually married to an impetuous young girl. A girl-woman that gave 'me' and my sister life, and was living in Long Branch. The birth of these two youngsters would turn out to be a terrifying and unsafe place for many decades.

So, the eternally overwhelming and awkwardly repetitive questions will always be: "Was he indeed a Greek priest? Was he a con artist? Why did he leave so many places in such a hurry and always angry? Was he in trouble with the law? Why did he have such a secret life? Why did he literarily drag us around every so often to then dump us, only to 'undump' us when the insane mood overtook him?

Why was he unable to be a father, or at the very least, be a kind person? Why didn't he ever look 'me' in the face? Why was a conversation with him never possible? What did he do in the years he left us? Where did he go? Where did his money come from? What was the truth about Sophie and John?"

I know some of these questions have been vaguely touched on already. Maybe he was just a very disturbed man from the beginning of his impenetrable life, a person in need of help, a lost soul, and a being he never found or even knew he was lost. Whatever the answers: there can absolutely be no valid excuses, for how he lived and what he was and wasn't.

At some point my sister had moved to Bakersfield with her two young boys and somehow, by what means do not know, but that man called my Papa went to live with them. For how long, I do not know. But they knew each other because they had lived their unconventional lives together in Utica, New York, in San Francisco, and lastly Bakersfield. Obviously they kept in touch somehow.

For 'me' his whereabouts were never known, and accordingly of no concern as I was of no concern to him. "And isn't that a sad commentary." The mysterious John Leonides never ceased to be an unpredictable puzzle, and a compulsively abusive, addicted, human entity who disappeared and abandoned 'me' for long periods and too many times to even conjure up.

My sister did not choose to talk about their unusual life together or her life or my life. She would not have been interested in this book overflowing with my tender tears, fear, uncertainty, and questions but ultimately would end up for 'me' with happiness and contentment. "This makes 'me' sad beyond describable words."

When David and I had been married less than a turbulent year, the doorbell buzzed one evening in our little Chestnut Street apartment. In answering it, there stood somewhat of a human being: "I am your Papa." I hadn't seen him since I was thirteen (well over a decade plus), and I began to shake. David came up alongside of 'me', softly whispering in my ear: "Your father can't take you away again, don't be afraid, my Margie, you are a grown woman, you are married, we are married, you are my wife."

He had very little to say or share, but insisted on taking us, as we walked in silence, to a depressing cafeteria, on the south side of Market Street, for a dismal meal. David and I kept screening for even one explanation of this strange and unexpected visit after so many uncaring years. "How did he even know where to find 'me'?"

So, aha, finally he asked, with no compunctions or sense of pride, for money to go back to his birthplace in Greece. He confessed he wanted to end his days there. I believe he loved his homeland, possibly the only thing he ever loved. David and I were barely able to scratch for ourselves, and so there was no money to dole out, and if there had been: "Would I have given him what he blatantly ask of 'me', a stranger, a nothing to him? A castaway?"

He walked away from us as unexpectedly as he came and, and in his usual disregard, he left without a word, a touch, or even a smile. He asked nothing about my life, nor cared. He did not choose to discuss his own life. The last poignant glimpse of him that I could summon up with any amount of compassion was the vision of him, hunched as he slowly and unemotionally walked again, out of my life. I never saw or heard from him again, ever. "There is no place in my heart to care or to know how or when he returned to his birthplace."

He was not a ten-foot tall man to be feared, after all, but only five-nine. He was a person who went to bed one lustful night, as a young, eager man, with a seemingly innocent but conniving girl, who was the person that gave me the gift of life.

"Perhaps there should be gratitude in 'me' for her and for him. That's a hard one. Can't go there."

All it took was one self-centered night of their irresponsible love making, and it resulted in the fruitless sum and total of our nothing loveless relationship.

Even so, empathy for such a person, as he shuffled away, truly filled 'me.' This once terrifying creature was a stranger to 'me', and I was equally and sadly a stranger to him.

"He missed so much, what was he searching for in his sorry life? Who was he? Not a good man, not a bad man, not an honest man, not a loving man, but without a doubt a completely selfish, self absorbed man with no understanding to give anyone. Or perhaps he was simply a lost, bewildered and disturbed spirit, who in this day and age might have been fortunate to find some medical help. More than likely he would not even have recognized his disquieting evil qualities."

When preparing to write my one woman show sometime in the nineties – a show that took five years to research, write, and finally bring into fruition – there was, in 'me', a compelling, an almost overwhelming, need to board a plane bound for Greece, to look into more of this unkind and disturbed man who insisted we call him Papa.

I never had even the slightest desire to search out Sophie's life because of all the palpable reasons so written in this story. Frankly I could not bear to know anything more of this poisonous human being. A person that utterly failed completely, as a mother, perhaps even as a person. She was a child/woman whose young body I came out of so many decades ago, and as said, earlier:

"That was the substance of our nothing relationship." She was not a mother to 'me,' and I was not a daughter to her. Regretfully we balanced each other out.

There wasn't much to discover about my father in his village of Plantonos, Greece. I met his sister Olga's daughter, my first cousin Victoria, and that was a giant plus.

There was a small section of terraced property that belonged to his family. As for the plot that was to be his, he selfishly and recklessly gambled it away in one night of total drunken wildness. Victoria is still very angry about this, one of his many selfish, disrespectful acts.

The school he attended as a child was touching to peek into. I pushed my imagination to possibly envision him sitting at one of the quaint little wooden desks, when he was a tussled haired, blameless and possibly lovable child.

The historical church his father headed for years was truly awe-inspiring. The grandiose of the miniature cathedral sent many goose pimples to coolly trickle down my arched back.

This was over a century old picturesque stone edifice that hundreds of people solemnly entered to worship in their private ways. Each mortal seeking forgiveness and ultimately peace of soul.

Victoria and I dejectedly walked by the small, old-fashioned village house he lived in during his last years. It would have been heartbreaking, and also creepy, to wander inside. To perhaps feel his dark presence, plus the many unsettling emotions, be they good or bad. "Was my father an embarrassment, Victoria?"

"No, Margie, he drank too much while dancing and singing all night by himself and then slept his days away in oblivion. That was his life here, and then he died. Maybe that's why you love to sing and dance."

"Do you know your real name? It is Margarete Mavrothalassites, not Leonides." What a stunning shock when she told me that in her hard to understand but delightful accent (much like my Thea's). My response, without a moment of hesitation: "Thank God I didn't know that in school. How would those unkind and tormenting orphans, at St. Vincent's home, have ridiculed that long and difficult name? Leonides was bad enough. Don't even want to know how to spell it." (Which in time I did find out and here it is).

HERE'S TO YOU

Lyrics by Margie Belrose
Dedicated to Davy and Dea Belrose

HERE'S TO YOU HERE'S TO ME MAY WE NEVER DISAGREE

HERE'S TO TASTING THE STARS AS THEY SPARKLE FOR A

TRILLION MILES

AND NO MATTER WHERE WE GO, WE'LL HAVE TO TRAVEL

VERY FAR

AND STILL WE'LL NEVER REACH THOSE GLEAMING STARS

TO TASTE THEIR PROMISED LOVELINESS

HERE'S TO ME HERE'S TO YOU

LET'S REACH OUT TO MAYBE TASTE THE STARS AS THEY

SHINE THROUGH

NIGHT AFTER NIGHT AFTER NIGHT AFTER NIGHT

OH WHAT BEAUTY THEY PROMISE YOU AND ME

SO HERE'S TO YOU HERE'S TO ME

MAY WE NEVER DISAGREE

I'M SO GLAD WE ARE THREE

AS WE WATCH THOSE TWINKLINGS STARS

A TRILLION MILES FROM HERE

SCENE THIRTY-TWO

To further find out about my mystifying, neglected young life of abuse, and terror, a plane flew me directly to Saginaw and then over to Detroit, to hopefully see, one more apprehensive time, the orphanages.

To my astonished and tearful disbelief, and forever-profound disappointment, they both were gone. "Oh, I should have traveled back there years ago." Where the big dark scary brick building of St. Vincent's once stood, my uncompromising dream was to walk in the over-size wooden front doors and to sit on the window seat where the only doll in my life, ever, was placed in my tiny arms by caring Sister Theresa, and where I hid my ball of used gum.

I wanted so much to see where we all slept and ate. Where the old fashion bathtub stood to take my warm weekly bath while wearing a towel around my waist, and severely told, many times over: "Never touch yourself, it is a sin." To see the narrow, single spring bed that Sister Theresa lovingly tucked 'me' in when covered with itchy hives, to see the play yard, that was long gone, and where the young blond boy, Carl, had kissed my hand after racing to capture my rolling tire. To see and be touched by the sacred chapel that had to be dusted every day with great reverence. "Maybe by some unexplained miracle there would be that same beautiful Sister Theresa, who was the first person to overtly care about 'the me,' such a scared little girl. She, with little knowledge, turned my life around forever more, with a simple warm emotion called "LOVE."

And what had happened to my daily cruel tormentor, Sister Mary Matthew? What stared back at my bewildered and stunned face was an empty, not very large, area, with no playthings, just a somewhat small ball playing lot.

"How could a big, menacing brick structure stand on what now seemed like such an insignificant scrap of land? How could it be gone? How could the once sinister building be demolished and imploded?" I would have cried out: "wait, wait, let me find my doll and my ball of gum, please wait. Where is Sister Theresa?" Was there no one there with a compassionate heart to hear the mighty thud as it toppled to the unforgiving ground that held such a building up for over a half century plus?" Sorrow filled my very essence as a few salty tears trickled down my face. Nightly when I long for sleep, I beg the sorrow to go away.

It helped to find St. Vincent's summer camp at Shields Landing, and to stand in the very corner of the fence, that was amazingly still strongly upright, where thoughtless torments and ridicule were ruthlessly lashed out at 'me' from children who were more than likely as emotionally damaged as 'the me' was. Therefore I was bound to become the substance of their displaced revenge and anger.

Then to slowly walk over to the sweet little grotto where there no longer stood a statue of the Virgin Mary and where there no longer were 'devil snakes', and could rightly never again be called a grotto. It took a moment remembering the 'devil snake' "Where was the very big swimming pool? Why can't the gleeful laughs of the staid nuns be ever heard again?"

Where the pool once invitingly gleamed, all that remained was the plumbing teasingly sticking out of the hard ground. Why would anyone throw away such a swimming pool? My logic says, "if it was broken, why not just fix it?"

Maybe someone would take but a smidgen of time to find
a scrapbook of pictures hidden away, or could tell 'me' what
had happened to the loving as well as the unloving nuns. But
remorsefully, it had been over four decades and there was no one
diligently working or walking around. Who could possibly know or
imagine what this once upon a time orphan was looking for, talking
about, or pining for in her deepest place?

How could they know of the ominous St. Vincent's that still sadly
clung in my memory, the St. Vincent's that held both happy and
unhappy memories for 'the me' that was no longer an unhappy and
cruelly treated abandoned child?

It was St. Vincent's that my heart desperately longed to see and
feel once again. Whatever emotions might be trying to push out, it
would be good to feel, to cry about, and might even feel joy about.
"There had to have been some measure of happiness there in all
those years, in a place that spelled terror for 'me' every day while
living in a world of abuse. But yes there was that little bit of LOVE
that saved my very being and ailing heart."

In Detroit, the Protestant Asylum no longer stood there either,
and in its place a cheap, depressed motel looked out at a world
that no longer cared. "What happened to all the children in that
asylum, who were so much like myself, 'the me' that once was? What
happened to the little birdlike naked child?"

Though 'the me' tried to share all of this with Ethel, all these
adventures and feelings, as always, she did not want to know any of it:
my trip to Greece, to Michigan, to my life. She did not want to know
'the me' I have never stopped searching for. If still alive, she would

not have been interested in the writing of this book. She would have carelessly shoved it aside and 'me' again. "Was she looking for her own self at any time along her dejected way? We might have been able to find ourselves while crying sadly together, and that would have been nice, truly nice and good for our very souls."

As said earlier, Ethel changed her first name five times, detesting her given name of Ethel, even though I would tell her of all the famous people with her same name. She was inadvertently trying to discover herself in some hopeful way by doing that. Then she might be happy, or at the least find a modicum of contentment. Aunt Toni, one of the five names she picked, is what my young family chose to call her. After all, my sister was their aunt, and they loved her. But she never could recognize nor feel their undemanding sweetness they unselfishly tried to wrap around her.

There was a time she called herself my daughter's name, Dea. Learning of this it made 'me' infuriated with her. She needed so much to have what was mine, even to assume my daughter's exceptional name.

After my livid letter to her, she instinctively knew she had to change her name again; I don't remember to which one.

Toni was always cleverly amusing in telling stories with great accents, but more often than not, she would rather choose to sit in a confined position of self-pity, demanding your unqualified attention. "Toni, find a theatre company in the East Bay (where she lived) because you have some talent, go discover it" But her life of incredible damage so permeated the very fundamental nature of her tainted being she was visibly a sad tragedy to watch. She was unable to reach out and change her life to then plant her feet on a positive path that might possibly have set her free.

No one could lovingly touch her. It was near to difficult to call upon the healing emotion to like her because she made no attempt to like you. Even so, there was empathetic love from 'me' for her always, though it was pernicious at times. The termination of her very broken psyche was catastrophically complete from very early on. She was unable to see it, did not realize it, and was paralyzed in not being able to change it. "What a sorrow, what a tragic human waste. The likelihood of goodness, sweetness, and unconditional love would forever elude her."

Of course my childhood was one of a very tender and terrified child also, who was neglected, horrifically punished, maliciously invalidated, and abandoned many times over. But LOVE from Sister Theresa, Dorcus, my Thea, and the Ferrone family had miraculously and generously entered my life at various times and that LOVE made my life grossly dissimilar to my damaged sister's.

However, the experiences we both suffered through could not begin to compare to the tragedies that were being unbelievably foisted upon millions of children, and their parents, in Europe, at the same time as my own young life was seemingly tragic beyond words. Everything, just everything, is exclusive to each human being, wherever they might be in this, more often than not, glorious world. So, for whatever it is worth, this Margie person has been a "lucky duck" and cannot help but feel pain and unspeakable compassion for all the neglected and abandoned children living in every corner of our planet, then and now. In spite of it so often being said that "all things are relative" there is guilt in 'me' to think and know my life was and is a "bowl of cherries." Seems not quite fair to them.

I AM GRATEFUL

Lyrics by Margie Belrose
Dedicated to Davida Herwin

I AM GRATEFUL FOR ALMOST EVERYTHING
THOUGH THAT DOESN'T SEEM A POSSIBILITY
THE TREES ACHING TO REACH THE SKY
THE BIRDS THAT FLY INCREDIBLY HIGH
THE LITTLE BABIES THAT CRY AND CRY
THE SWEETNESS OF EACH DAY GONE BY
THE ABILITY WE ALL HAVE TO SURVIVE
I AM GRATEFUL FOR MY HOME
EVEN WHEN LEFT ALONE
I THEN LOOK AT MY BOOKS AND PICTURES
AND I AM NOT ALONE
MY TREASURES ARE SO MUCH A PART OF MY HOME
AND LISTENING TO MUSIC, OH HOW IT ALL
INSPIRES MY CREATIVE JUICES
HOW COULD I POSSIBLY BE ALONE
WHAT A WORLD WE HAVE TO BE SO GRATEFUL FOR
IF THEY'RE JUST WERE NO WARS
IF THE HARMONY WE ALL LONG FOR
COULD START EACH DAY WITH A SONG
FULL OF JOY AND THEN WHAT MORE
COULD WE ASK FOR
WHAT MORE COULD WE BE

MAKING CHOICES

Lyrics by Margie Belrose
Dedicated to my sad and intolerably complicated sister

LIFE IS JUST A MATTER OF MAKING CHOICES,

GOOD AND BAD WE ALMOST GO MAD

THE CHOICES CAN TURN HAPPY AND OFTEN SAD

WHAT SHOULD WE DO TO SEE IT THROUGH

RIGHT OR LEFT UP OR DOWN

WE JUST KEEP GOING ROUND AND ROUND

LIFE IS JUST A MATTER OF MAKING CHOICES

WISE ONE DAY, WHO CAN SAY WHAT

IS RIGHT OR WRONG

WE'VE GOT TO BE STRONG TO GET ALONG

YOU COULD SING A SONG

AS LIFE IS JUST A MATTER OF MAKING CHOICES

SOME DAYS TURN HAPPY, SOME TURN SAD

IN THE END, WHY NOT JUST BE GLAD

SO CROSS YOUR FINGERS IN THE HOPE

YOU WILL BE WISE AND NOT A DOPEY DOPE

AS LIFE IS SIMPLY A MATTER OF MAKING CHOICES

YES IT IS, OH YES IT IS

© 2009 Margie Belrose

SCENE THIRTY-THREE

Through the years people have so often asked, "Why have you never remarried?" They express their curiosity with more than a semblance of pity in their tone of voice. What they do not distinguish is that it has always been my choice. There has been my professional and business life to be duly considered and two precious children to raise and watch over. So WHY?

Of course, have had my minor share of romances, several very serious ones, and several to married men and others. "Was I nuts? Yes. What was I thinking? I wasn't. What did I hope for?" This, in your eyes, might seem possibly disgraceful behavior on my part in some instances. Most of these dilly-dallying affairs occurred within a few years after the sudden departure of David. He had not shared his love, nor caressed 'me' passionately or otherwise, for long periods of time, longer than can be remembered. The questions that screamed out at 'me' so often: "Who was I? Was I a desirable woman, special in any man's eyes and heart? Was I to ever be loved again as a cherished woman?"

But to marry was an event that could not be, nor could 'the me' envision anyone who would willingly share my problematical life. It would not be fair to a possible partner, in fact it would be very unfair. "Oh, that doesn't mean I would not like to have a companion even now at this point in my twilight years, someone to share mutual respect, someone to snuggle with, to share platonic love, but to marry is not a pleasure that could be, as I see it."

Besides- who would want a woman, albeit a very beautiful and talented one, and of course successful (now this is a joke Charlie) who has three slight interweaving businesses to glue together as I energetically tap dance as fast, really fast, each day just to maintain? I cannot forget the impossible time as well as financial commitment they all selfishly demand, and two children who are adored in my heart above anyone.

It is hard to even find the elusive opportunity to clean my shower. Is there a joke here? "When this book is on the bookshelves of at least a few book stores, I will have my way with that shower and it will have its deserved day."

I had an artistic (not financial) partner for over a quarter of a century (good grief that is a long time). It began as a very, very brief, casual, non-committal romance between us very foolish sillies. But we could not be partners, and such a relationship did not survive the incredulous problems and decisions. This man's name is Damien. During most of that twenty-eight year period of time, he lived in various parts of the theatre, or sometimes not here at all.

He is an admired actor, writer, set designer and builder, a lighting expert, an intelligent man with a degree in theatre arts. He was artistic and a sometimes companion when it suited him. Everyone applauded his various talents.

"Was it obvious to 'me' all those productive years that he was also a completely selfish, sarcastic and narcissistic person with no empathy for anyone?" No, because it was imperative to ignore such bad behavior, primarily because of ongoing projects. He often deliberately made rude remarks to hurt 'me', always in front of people, ultimately destroying any possibility of their respect for 'me'.

In sorry retrospect, I know now, without question, he needed this theatre, not 'me'. My obsessed need was what he could offer this theatre, a win/win arrangement it would seem. I have tried to live (not always successfully, as it is hard) to see only the positive. What a chore that has been.

He often said, "You are my best friend." But I believe now, in thinking back, it was only for his wants at the moment. In the final analysis he left this lucrative and creative haven where he lived all those years with absolutely no financial responsibility. He was paid for everything he accomplished in this place called "The Belrose." He earned it.

In his defense, it must be acknowledged that he brought The Belrose Theatre that he jealously coveted for his own to a near professional level at times, and was dedicated and fervently involved in what he accomplished here. I would ask him a few times EVERY year, (deny this if you will, Damien), "Are you happy, do you want to make a change?" He would reply, "Yes, I am happy here and this is my stage."

More than fifteen years ago, on a Tuesday morning about ten a.m., he didn't seem quite right, a bit unsteady:

"Damien, are you drunk?"

"Yes I am."

"Have you become a functioning alcoholic?"

So with tough love rearing its' concerned head, "well, you have two choices. By Sunday you are out of here. You either go for rehabilitation or your things will be deposited on the sidewalk." "I don't have the money for help, it costs $3000."

"I am just your friend, call your mother in Pittsburgh."

He did, and the money came that very afternoon from far away Pittsburg. This man, barely able to hold his unsteady self together, left absolutely snockered on a Sunday, for his last hoorah, and the required 30 days of rehabilitation.

Had he not gone for help, the doctor told him he would have been dead in just a few months. "Hmmmm, wonder if he knows, with even a speck of gratitude, the chance of a continued life he was given by 'me', and clearly just in time by his doctors."

Without any warning, nor with a kind sit-down discussion, he announced one day in September of 2004 that he would be leaving to live with a woman that he barely knew, who headed a pot club. It was several weeks after the Belrose had a glorious anniversary of fifty years, where many hundreds of people from far and wide came to share such an eventful day. When asked, "Is this change you want to make for sex and drugs?" he simply answered, "Yes."

"Damien you should be ashamed of yourself." Within a few weeks he packed up and left in total. Damien and this woman planned to marry within a year, but the life of the torrid and quick affair was less than six months.

Putting my stupid pride in my stupid back pocket, I asked him to do one more project here. He did it reluctantly and then made his final, arrogant exit from the Belrose with a couple of caustic and unbelievable lies that could only end up in hurtful, bitter words between us, and unfortunately did.

It took six months and the delving into four inspirational books about forgiveness, and other spiritual values, to heal 'the me' emotionally from his betrayal. "Still not sure, I really have."

Because of the unkind way Damien left, and the mean tirade that came out of a mouth that had no kindness or respect in their tone, I have reinforced my staunch philosophy.

"It ain't what you do or say, it's the way that you do or say it." I really don't care that he left, "oh, sure I do", but it is HOW. "He done 'me' wrong." And that's the sum and total of it all. He could have left with grace, been nice and kind, but I don't believe he has it in him or knows how. The hurt that he perpetrated on the Belrose family has cascaded into a very deep and dark place, and always will.

"Can Damien be forgiven? Possibly. Maybe not, and can I forget his unqualified disregard for the years he spent as my partner and so-called friend without looking back? Don't know. Time will tell." This again in my life was blatant abandonment, betrayal and desertion of the worst kind. This I had already lived through, so many heartbroken and distant years ago.

Thought this had all been mended, the billowing grey emotions of so long ago. Conceivably the haunting hurts of my childhood, though secretly tucked away for years in my psyche, may never really heal altogether to maybe disappear. However, I never stop working on that dreadful facet of my life. I was forced, by my own willing, eager and exciting choice, to write my play in the late nineties.

And of course now this very book, you are reading, to again revisit this 'stuff' and somehow work through it. This will happen, with much loving kindness to myself, and the return of a soothing peace that must be found in the depths of my being, and that I have with happiness, experienced in the past.

The following is being written after a kind mutual friend, Kenny Miles, felt Damien and I should try to put this hurt, for 'me' behind us both. So with respect for Kenny and his concerns, Damien and I have talked for a few hours.

There is so much more to plough through, if ever again (don't think so). The conversation brought out that Damien has serious emotional and mental problems from his experiences in the Vietnam War and being a spy in such a horrific conflict (which he never confided in 'me' about).

His doctors of the Veterans Administration advised him that without medication he really would be quite crazy, out of control and possibly dead. Many of the things we spoke of that day he said he cannot remember and denies ever doing or saying. Hmmmm.

He truthfully admitted he has no empathy for others, as a result of his war years. Damien is on total disability. He now says he feels sorry for all that was said and done, though he cannot remember most of it. Hmmmm.

Therefore, forgiveness for him must be in my heart and the hearts of my children. For 'the me', there is still a long road to travel on this zigzagging path, to heal wholly.

And so this ends the saga of Damien/Margie. There will be other discussions, maybe, but for now, the hurt in my heart, as so many other hurts, is slowly disappearing, as I am closer to

"The Me I Found."

ME ME ME

Lyrics by Margie Belrose
Dedicated to Damien

WHO WAS THE FIRST TO SAY ME ME ME
IT MUST HAVE BEEN ADAM,
IT COULD NOT HAVE BEEN EVE
MY WAY OR THE HIGHWAY
WAS THIS SAID BY ADAM IN A FIT OF ME ME ME
AS EVE WAS BUSY IN THE GARDEN OF EDEN
ENTICED BY THAT SNAKE TO EAT OF THE APPLE
THAT SEEMED TO SAY
COME AND TAKE A BITE OF ME
WAS ADAM THE BADDY, OH NO NO,
HE COULD NOT BE
IT MUST HAVE BEEN THAT SNAKE
THAT TEMPTED THEM BOTH
AND WHO TAUGHT ADAM TO SAY ME ME
GO AND SEE WHAT YOU CAN BE
DON'T EVEN THINK ABOUT EVE
HE TAUGHT ADAM TO SELFISHLY THINK OF ME
AND WHERE DID THAT LEAVE EVE?
PERHAPS TO FIND HER OWN ME ME, BUT GENTLER, SOFTER
AND MAYBE TO FIND A SPECIAL ONE
TO MAYBE SET ME FREE

SCENE THIRTY-FOUR

To review a few things that might have been lost in the shuffle: my concerted effort has been to pull things together from a life that has been beyond fragmentation from the onset and has been seemingly unorganized. And quite frankly difficult. I ask myself, "Margie, should you even have attempted this book?" I am uncertain about so many instances and scenes it is driving 'the me' near nutso.

But nevertheless, here is another scene, if you will.

My two adult children are so very kind, thoughtful and the sweetest people ever. "Could I possibly be prejudiced? Yep."

I am fortunate to have them in my life. Would love them even if they weren't my generous gift. They are just good people. Somehow along my scraggly travels, on this pothole-filled road, goodness was learned and consequently taught to the two souls loaned to 'me' for my circuitous stay on this ever-changing earth.

Principally from Sister Theresa, Dorcus Holt, my Thea, the Papalias family, the Kahns, the Ferrones. And many others maybe even YOU.

A few more disjointed thoughts, perhaps touching on redundancy. Maybe it will be like re-winding "Are you still with me?"

The costume shop has acquired (by what means exactly am not sure) hundreds of renaissance costumes and we are fortunate to be associated with seven faires across the country. We have built our own quaint cottages, and also have one very large tent shared at two faire sites for costume rentals. The costumes are all freighted from faire to faire. Son David thinks we have about 600 renaissance rental costumes.

"Good grief how did that happen, where did they all come from? Not sure." Davy handles and manages all of this. The logistics of this part of our business are mind-boggling, but my very organized Virgo son has been doing it for years. A few ups and downs in the beginning learning years, but now, though he has to travel a lot, he has it all buttoned down tightly.

The rentals from these faires are candidly what gratefully maintain the financial life of The Belrose. Davy and I are in business together. When we talk business he calls me Margie, not Mom, and to 'me' he is David, not Davy. (Dea doesn't like that). And when we just talk, not business, he calls 'me' Hony Mom (this a name Dea coined years ago) and he is my Davy baby, and that is a name he called himself as a young child. (Is that silly or what?) When my daughter and 'the me,' just talk business or otherwise, it is Mom, because we two are also in business together.

Davy works part-time for his late father's song writing partner Don Deane, who owns a picturesque bar and hotel in the coastal town of Bolinas. He crunches numbers, manages things for Don and is his true and trusted loyal forever friend.

In addition to this he manages the seven renaissance faires, which could be a bit much. Of course he has his family and home to love and take care of too, and he does.

Must talk further about Davy for a moment.

As a young boy, handsome Davy studied dance and acting classes with his father and 'me'. He loved studying the drums and then he in turn, was able to teach drums, and of course played for many of our shows when he wasn't performing as an actor. He had loads of girlfriends who vied for the affections of the tall, slender, talented, and very good-looking young man that is my son.

He was a track star and football player in junior high. I never liked him playing football because the thought of a possible injury always set me on a slippery edge, but he did it, was good at it and remained unscathed.

When David died, Davy was just entering his freshman year by one month, and was lost in every imaginable way, confused, making many stupid mistakes, and no longer played sports. He did get through high school with passable grades, and then two years of junior college. The story of the comedy club has been sullenly told earlier. After the club went south, Davy suffered a depression that lasted for untold months.

STAGE THIRTY-FIVE

Now to talk about my lovable daughter, a five hundred year old soul that would exclusively be named Dea Marcene Belrose. She was born on a marvelous sun-filled morning that was ever lightly approaching a foggy day, called November twenty-fifth, 1958. It was near Thanksgiving, and I am forever thankful.

She and Davy together studied dance and acting, with both David and I, during all their young formative years. As mentioned earlier, she went to U.C.L.A. on a partial scholarship at seventeen and majored in theatre arts.

At that time a student couldn't take acting and dance there. It was one or the other. Dea ended up taking dance classes at various studios in Los Angeles, some good ones, some she had to escape from.

Her strength has always been tap, but she is an accomplished and very appealing jazz dancer. From a young age she was a sensitive, and just plain good actress. She took piano lessons, and, as her teacher expressed with much hope: "If Dea wants to be a fine pianist, she has the talent." Nope, Dea wanted to dance and act, and to just study the piano entirely was not to be in her future.

Winning on the Gong Show was a real coup for her as was her career with the famed American Folk Ballet. You can Google "Dea Belrose" and watch her two-and-a-half minute tap dance she won on the Gong Show. "Oh god, she was such a cutie on that popular show of its' day."

Dea taught dance classes while a student at U.C.L.A. for a city recreation department. She worked in a pizza store and cleaned a house or two to make ends meet. At times 'the me' finagled a few bucks to send her in order to save her 'a**'.

She now continues to teach tap here at the Belrose and sometimes performs. She is extremely patient and kind in her expertise and style of teaching. She lends her input in our productions and given enough time she would be more involved, but am so grateful for what she does contribute, which is always intelligent and creative.

She has a partner, Joanne, and earns her livelihood as the manager of Joanne's Print Shop in Sausalito, just twelve minutes from 'me'. They printed this very book you are reading this very lazy daisy day. She, like Davy, is organized and successfully puts one dancing foot in front of the other each day. She is a hard worker, and is a forever joy. We are compelled to talk several times daily. "What would happen to 'the me' without hearing their voices every day? Can't entertain that thought, so I won't."

My two charges, my miraculous gifts, tell their hony mom that they are happy, and they look happy; therefore, this person, their loving lifetime caretaker is happy.

They each have their own productive and creative lives of course, and that's the way it must be. We will always remain close. Can't be any other way.

IT'S ALL UP FOR GRABS
Lyrics by Margie Belrose
Music by Jim Shelburne
Dedicated to those with dreams

I'M NOT REALLY WHAT I SEEM TO BE

I THINK THERE'S AN ACTRESS IN ME

I HAVE GLADNESS I HAVE SADNESS

I AM NOTHING THAT I SEEM TO BE

I AM CRYING IT'S WHAT I WANT TO DO

I JUST WANT TO CRY

I AM LAUGHING IT'S WHAT I DO

I JUST WANT TO LAUGH

I LOVE EACH DAY I CARE ABOUT ALL I SEE

AND SAY

BUT WHAT DOES IT ALL MEAN WHEN IT IS SAID AND DONE

I CAN ONLY GUESS AH, THE RACE ISN'T WON

IT'S ALL UP FOR GRABS

SHALL I CRY NOW? SHALL I LAUGH?

SHALL I SAY, WELL IT'S ALL UP FOR GRABS

AT LEAST TODAY

NOT TOO BAD NOT TOO BAD I'D SAY

THAT'S JUST THE WAY THAT'S

WHY IT'S ALL UP FOR GRABS TODAY

SCENE THIRTY-SIX

And now for my very own life, other than what has already been sometimes painfully and often joyfully written within these scenes. According to this computer/monster, which I have a continuous love/hate relationship with there are over 68,000 words within these pages. Don't misunderstand, not 6,800, but 68,000. "Good grief, can that be true? "Well that's what this ****computer spits out."

My life has centered primarily on the Belrose theatrical school since 1954, the ever-changing theatre since 1962, the costume shop since 1978 and now the faires that maintain my financial a**. The school unfortunately is not experiencing its former heyday, when there was a minimum of two hundred students to teach each week (oh, did I love that?) There are just enough pupils now to keep the teacher in me only somewhat satisfied. I am still in touch with many of the students from the past, who actually have become my forever-loyal friends.

The school inadvertently now suffers from people planting their behinds in front of their computers with the internet, e-mail, T.V., texting, the crowded freeways, video games, both parents forced to work, high mortgages, divorces, some nearby schools closing, countless health clubs, soccer, oh good grief, that word: Hip-Hop.

The creative juices for many might possibly are being corrupted with video games, and then there is the scary economy, people moving north or out of state, possibly a lack of interest or inspiration, and maybe because of the technology of today. It is just a different world, a harrowing one for 'me', and maybe you too. If we don't keep out spirits up, it could be quite dismal, maybe even bleak. No, we cannot let that happen.

We were fortunate in 1954, to establish our school and being at the right time. This before the world was so problematic and before technology took over our creative lives and maybe even our souls. "Oh please, say it isn't so."

There are many hundreds of letters to and from friends and past students (some have left our world), but this loyal human you are reading about does not have it to throw any of these treasures away. I need to glance at a correspondence once in awhile just to be reminded of an endearing time and the close friendships that still survives after so very many years that have mysteriously run into decades.

My children, with possibly the same loyalty instilled in them by their father and mom, will have to take care of these sentimental tokens. "Kids, when I kick over, it will be your sensitive and thoughtfully revered job to do something about all these precious letters, cards, letters of acknowledgments, etc."

In my archival room there is a box titled "Life is not always a bowl of cherries." The file box I can no longer look into, that viciously holds some letters that are mean and rarely signed. They make 'the me' blue, and teary, at the same time forcing 'me' to look at myself objectively.

I think of the tired old cliché: "You can't please everyone." My ardent effort is to not let mean words, both written and spoken, affect me personally. "Not easy to do, as they invalidate 'me.'" But that cardboard container is only kept to remind 'me' to keep a healthy balance in my ever-changing life: The yin the yang, the good, the bad, the positive, the negative, and the irrepressible terrible.

The costume and prop shop live in the lower level of this exceptional theatre.

Along with the Renaissance Faires, they are what valiantly strive to keep the petite "Belrose Empire" buoyant, and my own task is to paddle in this mélange, in one spot, as frenetically as is possible, every new day. "Since my first love is being a teacher, what is this person doing renting and caring for 3000 costumes?" Well, it works with this theatre/world of mine, that fortunately came our way in 1962, and I've often been told, "What you do is an asset to this community."

It is easy to actually love many of the costumes, the materials, and the styles. Some of them have been given their own personal names. It works out just fine for the Belrose and my hurried and sometimes hysterical life. I have to tell you with all honesty: "I would not, could not, change for anything in this whole lovely upside down and so often crazy world, that has been both good and bad to 'the me', and probably to you too."

WALK WHERE I HAVE BEEN

Lyrics by Margie Belrose
Music by Gillian Lovejoy
Dedicated to the people who have hurt me
by their words, their letters, their disrespect

IF YOU WANT TO WALK WHERE I HAVE BEEN
WE'LL SIT DOWN AND MAYBE GET TO THE END
BUT BEFORE WE START OUR TREK
WE'LL BASK IN THE SUN THEN MOVE AHEAD
TO SAY THE THINGS THAT MUST BE SAID
SHALL WE START WITH SADNESS, GOODNESS OR FUN
WE COULD TALK OF HAPPY TEARS,
FEARS OR EVEN GLUM
THEN WHEN IT'S ALL OVER
WE'RE SURE TO FIND A FOUR-LEAF CLOVER
(MUSIC INTERLUDE)
AND THEN WE'LL MOVE AHEAD
AND SAY THE THINGS THAT MUST BE SAID
IF YOU WANT TO WALK WHERE I HAVE BEEN
WE'LL SIT DOWN AND DOWN AND COUNT THE
MEMORIES AGAIN, MAYBE EVEN GET TO TEN

SCENE THIRTY-SEVEN

At least four times a year, the question that must be asked of myself.

* "What show shall this theatre do next?" It bam bushels.
  (Is that a word?)

* "Will my decisions work, where will the performers
  come from, will anyone really care? Oh, God, what to do?"
  You would of course think that quick answers would be right on
  the tip of my slender fingers (that need a manicure) after all
  the shows since 1954 but the answers are just not there, aren't,
  aren't, aren't.
  Each project is exceptional, has a life of its own, and offers
  problems and stressful demands unique to them.

* The Marin Women's Hall of Fame for the Arts inducted 'the
  me' in 1996 "Could it possibly be that long ago?" Three talented
  women nominated 'the me'. "Was this the surprise and the
  honor of my life? YES." "Did Margie Belrose, the castaway I
  once knew and recognized as Margie Leonides, deserve such
  deference?"
  Gosh, I have been doing what I love all these years,
  No, all my life.
  So, if such an exceptional tribute drifted in my direction   as the
  result of tenacity, perseverance, sacrifice, love, passion and longevity,

then, "Yes, this honor is accepted with deep appreciation and humility. And thank you all."

🌸 My nominating trio was made up of writers, so I consequently spent three months composing my humble five-minute speech so Margie Belrose wouldn't embarrass them. "What would they think of this story?" A question asked of myself now. But unfortunately I will never know, as two of the talented and kind ladies no longer walk this earth: Dorothy Hughes and Alice Yarish. Their belief and respect for what has been lovingly accomplished here is something that shall always be close to my heart. Jeanne Samuelson, the third member of the trio, is fortunately still with us. That once-in-a-lifetime recognition was my academy award, my Tony, my Golden Globe.

To prepare for this most extraordinary of nights 'me' savored the playful but wise advice of my dear, ever-lovin' friend, Sue-Sue Finegan. "Now, Miss Margie, you have to do what the stars do. Get a facial, a massage, eyebrows shaped, a colonic (oops), double up on your vitamins, do your nails, toes, get hair colored, go to the dentist and smile, smile, smile."

And all these things were cognately done, allowing 'the me' to really experience what a star feels like on that one glorious evening, March 21, 1996. A moment in my life to never be repeated again. See, I am a lucky duck.

🌸 Shortly after, another recognition followed when asked to be included in a book, "100 Faces of Marin" by Peter Anderson.

This was also unexpected. Don't mean to brag, (oh, sure I do,") but these two honors have to be shared: How can I help it?

🌸 At this point in time, April, 2010, since this book has not yet been completed or published, but you are now reading this finished project, in spite of all the hoopla had to go thru with this book: I was recently notified and received the honor of being:

THE "CITIZEN OF THE YEAR AWARD 2010, FOR SAN RAFAEL, Truly another unexpected tribute. This new honor has now covered me with pink happiness and assures me that:

"YES I DO HAVE A HOMETOWN, I do, I do, I do.
Yep, I am a lucky duck, quack, quack, quack."

🌸 My own one-woman show "Stuff happens … and then" finally emerged after five years of blood, sweat, and tears (isn't that the name of a band?) Now that was terrifying.

"Where did the courage and the nerve come from?
Will anyone share such a night with me? Who will care, who will come?"

But it happened after many gut-wrenching and tearful months. "Or was it years? Yes it was years."

The process was one cathartic and agonizing remembrances after another. The show received two wonderful reviews. I could not believe it and it more than validated my adult life of sharing goodness.

"Can 'the me' be happy I did it? You bet. In fact, rather like what I am willingly and painfully struggling through writing this, for 'me', a momentous book. A daunting experience never contemplated in all my life. 'The me' cannot believe, even as I am coming to the end of this endeavor that the delicate task is finished."

HOW FAR IS A DREAM

Lyrics by Margie Belrose
Music by Jay Brower & Jim Shelburne
This is dedicated to Rachel Belrose
Who brought some of these lyrics to my attention
And is the adored daughter of her parents

HOW FAR IS A DREAM CAN YOU REALLY TELL

PERHAPS IT'S AS HIGH AS A STAR IN THE SKY

OR IS IT JUST A PILLOW AWAY

WILL YOUR DREAMS BRING FEAR OR SWEETNESS

WHEN NIGHTTIME CREEPS IN

WHEN YOUR MIND IS AT REST

WILL A DREAM COME YOUR WAY

BRINGING SWEETNESS TO MAKE A

WARM COZY NEST

HOW FAR IS A DREAM CAN YOU REALLY TELL

PERHAPS IT'S AS HIGH AS A STAR IN THE SKY

OR IS IT JUST A PILLOW AWAY

SCENE THIRTY-EIGHT
A TIME FOR THANKS

I give thanks every morning before my size six feet land on the carpet (that seems to always need cleaning) for so much, just so much. It is never ending.

✿ First, of course, escaping by the grace of the gods who have looked after 'the me' and who seem to be floating about, always protecting 'me', from the mentally sick mother and equally so, the father, who both, uncaringly announced to the world: "Here are two human beings, we don't want them, do what you will with them, who is to care, they are nothing."

The two irresponsible young people, who should never have been parents, but who in their ignorance, BRILLIANTLY taught 'me' what NOT to be.

✿ For being able to buy the Belrose building because of the belief in us, and the unselfish financial and moral help of Sol and Dorothy Abrams. For giving David, Margie, Davy and Dea, a chance to make a life. To have a life. To enable our impossible dreams to actually become a vivid reality.

Sadly, they both no longer are of this world that has now become so complicated. Oh wish they could see the changes here, and to give them many hugs and kisses of perpetual gratitude and to share so much with them.

❧ To the Ferrone family who unknowingly taught 'me' what a normal life is, along with unselfish love, for goodness and kindness. For rescuing 'me' just in the nick of time.

❧ To Stanley and Pat Kahn for teaching and guiding 'me' into the teacher and performer I longed to be and became, and for their endless giving generosity. They made my professional life possible. There is not enough love or respect for those two kind people.

❧ To philanthropic John Crystal who contributed a great deal to have a portion of our poor roof repaired, twice, and then helped with the purchase of our beautiful comfortable chairs and other generosities. Thank you, John. And it is known you have contributed a great deal to other projects. (You are really the beloved Charlie Chaplin to 'me').

❧ Robin Williams, for sending a substantial check to aid in paying the State Board of Equalization for taxes I did not even know were owed. For always thoughtfully remembering the Belrose family.

❧ To the late Thelley Preston for the second bathroom backstage she insisted be installed. (Good idea Thelley). She was a real patron of ours. Miss her very much.

❧ To Mary Lee Streble who has given oh-so-generously on several occasions, out of respect for what we have been doing for these many years. She was a student here at one time, a distinctively kind and talented human being, and a gifted musician. In a lovely sort of way, she has reminded me of Dorcus of so long ago, the first person to say, "I love you Margie."

❧ To the generosity of Phyllis and Max Thelan, who donated to our scholarship fund? It is well known they have been charitable to many other cultural causes.

- To the never-ending sweetness and giving of Pablo Castro for keeping our floors beautiful. Thank you, Pablo. You are a dear and kind man.

- To Clint Fischer, giving at one time, his help in countless ways, including the building of our balconies, along with Todd Hunter. I love those balconies, thank you both. But without the imagination and suggestion of Carlos Morales the balconies would never even have been thought of. So thank you Carlos for visualizing the possibilities of such a lovely addition.

- To Billy Brewster for literally hundreds of unselfish favors through many years, and being a true "Prince of a Man." A drummer here for over twenty years, and my life savior more times than can be enumerated.

- And to so many people. I cannot name them all for fear of leaving someone out.

BUT wait here are more:

- To gentle Wilfred George who came to my one-woman show. I did not know him at that time. But within weeks of meeting and talking to him, he donated big money and then in November of 2000, paid off my first mortgage of $38,000 through his charity fund.

    Very sadly, he no longer can be here. He went for a swim, climbed on his bike, started to peddle off, and suddenly fell over from a fatal heart attack.

    Some things in life are just not fair, not fair, and not fair. Will always miss this kindhearted man. He was a true philanthropist and quickly became my dear friend, and would have been my life long friend if the gods had given him just a bit more time on this earth.

❧ My forever friend Norma (unlike 'me,' she was David's intellectual buddy) had a M.A. in psychology—who moved from Marin to Santa Cruz many years ago, a caring woman that we kept constantly in touch with, by going to see her, by calling, by letters, by her coming to many Belrose productions.

She divorced, remarried and life financially was a full turn-around for her. Her second husband passed away after a few years into their marriage. He had successfully invested in stocks. About two years ago, 'the me' received a phone call from a friend in her home "Norma has had a stroke and left all of us."

Soon after, a letter arrived from a lawyer. My first reaction, "Oh, God, who is suing 'me'? What did I do wrong?" The letter was to advise my family we were in her will and trust. WOW. Not possible. Thought maybe a few thousand dollars to show her regard for 'me' and mine.

A year went by and just before the stocks took their tragic and merciless tumble in late 2008, a letter from an investment company was delivered. A great deal of junk mail floats in, so threw the letter out. But having second thoughts, reached in the trash and retrieved said letter. There was a check for over $165,000. Running, not walking, to the bank: "Is this real?"

Connected up with the greedy uncompromising mortgage company and in four days the impossible long standing, mortgage was paid off to the tune of $155,000, putting $10,000 in savings. **Soooooo, since 1962 there is no longer a feared Mortgage on The Belrose. I AM FREE FREE FREE.**

❧ "Will there ever be another Refinance? Oh, please, hope not." Well there is a small line of credit that with kindness stares at 'me' every month, but doesn't scare 'me'. But for now, yes, I am a lucky duck. Just one beautiful miracle after another. Thank you, Norma."

This all appears to be about that nasty but necessary thing of a special color green, by the name of "money."

Though it is hard to comprehend, and is appreciated beyond words, also more incredible are the friends made through the years who unselfishly contributed their talents, their help, their time, and their love to 'the me,' to this theatre, to my family.

None of this can be measured in money, in any amount of the dirty green stuff. It cannot be calculated in anything but affection, generosity, love, goodness, and loving kindness.

❀ This person Margie Belrose is filled with everlasting gratitude to so many for so much and my prayer goes out every morning to all that have made 'the me' their forever friend. Those of you that know 'me' please believe this to be the truth from the bottom of my gentle heart. Through the bittersweet experience in the writing of my one-woman show and now this book, and with my kind and loving children, and so much more, I am finally introduced face to face with.

THE ME I FOUND
And it makes me feel good. As I forgive oh so much!

PLEASE READ a bit more, it will be fun—I promise. >>>>>>

I'M FEELING GOOD

Music and Lyrics by Margie Belrose
Dedicated to the late and talented Gillian Lovejoy,

HOW DO YOU FEEL MY FRIEND ASKED
I'M FEELING GOOD JUST LIKE I SHOULD
ARE YOU BLUE OR SAD, MAYBE FEELING BAD
I'M FEELING GOOD JUST LIKE I SHOULD
WHEN THE SUN IS BRIGHT AND WARM
I JUST WANT TO GET ALONG
WHEN THE RAIN COMES DRIZZLING DOWN
I JUST WANT TO SING A SONG
HOW DO I FEEL WHEN I STROLL INTO TOWN
I LOOK AROUND AND IT MAKES ME FEEL GOOD
NO, I'M NOT FEELING BAD
NO, I'M NOT FEELING SAD
FEELING GOOD, I'M FEELING GOOD
I'M FEELING GOOD JUST LIKE I SHOULD
WHEN I LOOK AT THE STARS
SO FAR AWAY AND BRIGHT
AND I KNOW, REALLY KNOW IN MY VERY SOUL
THERE IS A SPIRIT WE CAN ALL LOOK TO AND CALL OUR
OWN
AND THAT MAKES ME FEEL GOOD JUST LIKE I SHOULD, JUST
LIKE I SHOULD, JUST LIKE WE SHOULD

DO BE DO

Lyrics by Margie Belrose
Music by Peter Pennhallow
Dedicated to Charlie

DO BE DO IS REALLY TO DO AND BE AND DO
SHAKESPEARE SAID
TO BE OR NOT TO BE
I SAY DO BE DO BE DO
LIVING FREE IS WHAT DO BE DO CAN DO FOR YOU
DO UNTO OTHERS AS YOU WANT YOUR BROTHERS
TO DO BE DO TO YOU
TO DO IS TO BE, SAYS SOCRATES
THAT'S JUST LIKE DO BE DO
WHEN THE WORLD IS UPSIDE DOWN
INSIDE OUT AND GOIN SOUTH
THE ROOM IS SPINNING ROUND
DO BE DO IS THE ANSWER I HAVE FOUND
DO BE DO IS THE ANSWER I HAVE FOUND
DO BE DO IS THE ANSWER I HAVE FOUND,
DO   BE   DO

© Margie Belrose 2009

TWO STEPS FORWARD
AND ONE STEP BACK

Lyrics by Margie Belrose

Music by Alan Young

Dedicated to the efforts of all of us who strive

TAKING TWO STEPS FORWARD
AND ONE STEP BACK
MUST SURELY BE THE STEPS TO TAKE
TO FIND THE ANSWERS FOR MY LIFE
TO FORGIVE TO FORGIVE AND LET IT REST
WHEN MY HEART IS LIGHT, NO NEED TO FIGHT
WHEN HARMONY AND PEACE SET IN
THAT'S HOW I'LL KNOW I'VE DONE MY BEST
JUST FORGIVE JUST FORGIVE AND LET IT REST
IF THE STEPS WE TAKE
DON'T MAKE US RICH OR FAMOUS
WHO CAN BLAME US
IF THESE SAME STEPS CAN HELP US FIND
OUR WAY
HOORAY, TAKING TWO STEPS FORWARD
AND ONE STEP BACK
MUST SURELY BE THE STEPS TO TAKE
TO FIND THE ANSWERS FOR MY LIFE
WHEN I WALK SOFTLY EACH DAY
AND REST PEACEFULLY EACH NIGHT
THEN I'LL KNOW THAT
TAKING TWO STEPS FORWARD
TWO STEPS FORWARD AND ONE STEP BACK
ARE THE STEPS TO TAKE

TID BITS

As thoughts randomly pop into this overloaded and very often wacky head of mine, not at all in the "organized" way this Virgo-Leo person does some things. So come, laugh, cry and share with 'the me' just a tidbit more.

Don't look for structure – it ain't here, oops, Charlie, mean "It isn't here" or anywhere in my first, and most likely only book.

- Dea called just out of her freshman year at U.C.L.A. and said, "I am going to leave school for a year."

  "No you are not, my darling child. Too many young people say and do the same thing, never to return to complete their education. So, my sweet, talented daughter, you will stay for your remaining three years."

  And she did indeed continue her schooling. She has been very quick to tell 'me' that much of what she was taught at the university is of no use to her; even the highly respected acting classes were a disappointment. "Was she sorry she went? Nope"

  Her father would have gazed at her with great admiration. She did what he tried so hard to do and could have with the same discipline his daughter achieved.

- When she enrolled in an A.C.T. summer program her teacher called 'me' (something they seldom do), saying, "Dea is so well trained I really can teach her very little."

- When first arriving in Los Angeles, Dea called, "They are having auditions for the Gong Show tomorrow at ten in the morning. What shall I do?" "Wasn't that in your plan? Then go at ten tomorrow."

  "I guess I better practice my shuffles."

"Darling, you long ago passed that. You will win, you choreographed a terrific routine, use your psycho-cybernetics. You can do it."

And, as I told you already, she did. It was certainly the highlight of her young life.

❀ There was a time when this person writing this book, was pretty fanatical about health foods, vitamins, etc. (I have mellowed, truly).

Davy was on the junior Bulldog football team (the sport did not want him to participate in). I was teaching a jazz class of about twelve students when he cautiously walked into the studio, exhausted and hungry. "Mom, I'm starving." In my somewhat obsessive health food mode, "Well there are raisins and nuts on the kitchen counter."

Everyone in the class stopped as Davy dropped his gear with a thud and slowly approached 'me', not in a menacing way exactly, but very determined.

"You don't understand, Mom. I need meat and potatoes."

"Ok, ok, ok Davy baby, just get my wallet, take some money and go to Joe's for meat and potatoes."

He came home happy and full. The children in the class saw a mother and her son in a very personal way.

❀ This is the same child who was told he had to go from that day on to the bathroom, that he was done with diapers.

"You see that Davy, that is food your body couldn't use. It is poison."

Our friend George was baby-sitting him. Davy went to the bathroom, called to George, pointed to the toilet bowl and said, "You know what that is, George?" "What is it, Davy?"

"It's food my body couldn't use and it's poison."

George anxiously waited to tell us about Davy's announcement when we returned from teaching at one of the middle schools.

🌼 Davy never crawled; he simply stood up one day and walked at nine months old. "That was the end of any tranquility in my life." One evening when washing dishes he came up behind 'me' at about one year old, and bit my behind.
"Would you like 'me' to come up behind you and bite your bottom Davy?"
He ran to get his doll and holster, not knowing whether to love his doll or shoot his Mommie, instead he stood there with both toys, looking with a question on his bewildered face, not quite crying.

🌼 About the same time in Davy's nine-month-old-life, he took a roll of aluminum paper and wrapped it all around everything while his father sat back and watched in amusement. I came home later to find his daddy, still sitting and admiring his young son's adventure of the day.

🌼 When Dea was not yet two years old this same friend George gifted her with a big doll with hair, not a soft cuddly doll, but one made of hard plastic.
Dea did not want to make friends at all with this new intruder in her life, so she took her scissors (the one with the rounded ends) and cut all of the hair off. Then she took lipstick and smeared it on the doll's face. She did not even want to give this new doll person in her life a name. She would not tell 'me', in all my clever questioning, why she had such a dislike for that doll.
"Was this very tall doll too much for her little body to manage? I don't know. Actually she much preferred stuffed animals, especially her 'bear bear'.

✿ Davy was on the track team and broke a record. Every few years he still goes to his old middle school to see if his record has ever been broken. As of now it hasn't. It's a feather in his cap, of course.

"My heart tells me that Davy makes this visit of many nostalgic remembrances to his old school out of respect for all the hours of dedicated coaching his father devoted to him and the happy experiences he jumbled through for two years there."

✿ While in third grade, Dea had a tremendous dislike for a particular boy — it was mutual.

My children had been taught to face their problems, and write them down, to choose their battles, punch a pillow, cry, talk out their unhappiness, take a time out, sit on the couch and think. So Dea wrote on a piece of paper the vilest things she could think of at that age about this boy. She folded it up into a tiny square and put it in a corner of her closed desk.

For some unknown reason, her teacher went into her desk, found Dea's mini journal, if you will, and called 'me' in, displaying the paper of intense anger, to my amused eyes.

"What are you going to do about this?"

Could hardly contain myself, but in my most controlled and dignified manner I said, "I am not going to do anything about it and neither are you. Dea didn't punch his lights out, and she could have.

She didn't scribble terrible things on a wall in the bathroom, or on a fence somewhere. Dea wrote her feelings down privately, and you went into her desk and found it. Why would you go into her desk that is hers for the year? So maybe the principal should hear about the sneaky thing you did."

Oh dear, I have looked and looked for that paper to frame it and give it to my feisty kid, but it is nowhere to be found. I'm sure the teacher threw it away in her fury.

Dea was such an extraordinary child. She played in her mesh playpen for two years while my life was teaching for hours. But early one day she emphatically announced, "Out Mommie, out." Parents and students alike took pleasure in looking out after her while the hours of teaching went on, as did her father and Davy. Often 'the me' would give her a dish of cottage cheese, and what she managed to spill on the floor, our dog Nanette would come along and clean it up. Love those memories.

Davy had the same teacher for two years. They too, did not like each other. Coming home one day he was excited to tell 'me': "I watched Mrs. Bearsh today and she has over 30 tics in her face and body." (That was a day he surely learned nothing). It cannot be denied Davy had a good-sized chip on his shoulder that was stuck there for many years. Now it is only about an inch thick instead of being the familiar two-by-four we observed so often. But did he really have such a chip? Some people don't cotton to that in a person and neither did his teacher. "Is his mother proud of how he always did and can take care of himself and his family? You bet."

After Dea won the Gong Show, she was promised this and that, nothing wonderful. She called one day from L.A. "Mom, you know I am supposed to get a waffle iron as one of my gifts."

Grabbing up all my wisdom, "Dea, if you had a waffle iron would you use it?" "No." "I rest my case."

Actually, several years ago found one of about the same vintage. "Has she used it?" "Nope."

It sits on a shelf in her home along with other vintage treasures.

🌸 Three years before David didn't get a chance to say goodbye, I secured a morning job as a teacher's aide at a local middle school, teaching jazz dance in the P.E. Department. I needed to be away from here a few hours a day, to know what could be in the outside world, not just in my beloved theatre and school.

I was still working mornings there when he left us. My verbal agreement with the principal was to stay through the school year, but by mid-semester of that awful year, I told him the time had come to leave the job.

Up to that point, I had not yet gone through all of David's stuff. It needed to be done. It was time to put so many things in their place physically and emotionally to close this sad scene of my lonely life.

🌸 The lower level of the theatre was another teaching area for dance, drama and voice. Well, after David's passing the need for what it had been was no longer. It became a sort of a temporary storage and work area.

Rich Frost, who had been the bass player in David's easy rock band, made a little sleeping area for himself and lived there for some time. He used my kitchen and bathroom, eventually moved, found a life and married. We will always be friends.

He was here the morning David died, giving him mouth to mouth to no avail. He protected my two wide-eyed, frightened children until I could anxiously get back from the hospital.

"I never saw anyone who could eat so many mashed potatoes at one sitting. He was a poor and hungry boy."

🌼 The band, the Baltimore Steam Packet, played for The Belrose theatrical school's fiftieth anniversary in 2004. During that unusual day, several hundred people from far and wide, were in and out. So many memories, so much affection and concern for each other, endless sweet tears and hugs.

It was wonderful, a day never to be repeated, it was that magical with the Steam Packet playing, Rich, Carol, Dennis, Mark.

🌼 David had a small insurance policy. It paid off a few bills and a portion was for Davy to buy a high-end drum set. The manager of Drum Land called: "In all my experience there has never been such a polite young person to come into my store." Some of the dollars were used to split the lower level in half, a space we always called "Studio B", leaving one side for teaching, and making the other side into an apartment with the hope of it becoming an added income: (now, that's a joke).

It had two bedrooms, a front room, bathroom, kitchen and a gas fireplace. Very cute. For about six months it did get rented to two girls for real money.

🌼 When they moved, Damien made it his home for awhile, followed by a string of people in and out, including Davy and Dea. No one was ever charged. It did not become an income revenue source. Damn.

Not long ago, the count for all the people who made their digs in this building from time to time (some a long time) oh let's see, came to somewhere around forty five, give or take. Maybe you who are reading this book are one of them.

✿ As Davy and his wife-to-be, Cece, went out the door (they lived here too) to a big rented truck on their way to Omaha. A piece of plywood was already being taken down. Davy in disbelief: "I have the feeling I'm not welcome back."

"Not to live, my son, but no matter what happens, this will always be your home. Now you are on your way to a new life." We both cried and they drove off. In less than five minutes the big U-Haul truck came back. Davy was still crying and still needing to say another goodbye with very tight long hugs. My tender heart broke and stayed broken for the seven years he was gone.

✿ Davy moved with Cece to her hometown of Omaha, the hometown of Fred Astaire. He quickly secured a job with the Red Lion Inn as a food and beverage manager and found a father figure in his boss, Mr. Swanson.

When this kind father substitute left the Red Lion to take a similar job in Houston, Texas, he placed an urgent call to Davy, telling him he was needed and to please join him there. Not long after, Mr. Swanson left to go to Santa Fe, New Mexico, again taking Davy with him.

Santa Fe was not the place for Davy. Cece finally got pregnant (a very happy event). Davy called,

✿ "I need to come home and have this baby near you." They did, but were unable to find an affordable home in his beloved hometown of San Rafael, so they moved one-hour away and were able to settle in and buy an attractive house there.

It was just before then that Davy got involved with our faires, and also working for Don Deane. He found time to dash here to perform in a number of shows: playing Richard the Lion Heart for three seasons, and drumming for my own one-woman show.

In June of 2009 Davy and Cece's daughter, my granddaughter Rachel turned sixteen and became a junior in high school, an honor student. She now drives. (Good grief, not possible). They are a cohesive and loving family.

It was amazing to 'me' when Dea moved to Los Angeles and found her way on the complicated and actually terrifying freeways in just a week.

She then sorted her way through the very, very, very large U.C.L.A. campus, registering and all that means. And, good grief the library was so gigantic and bewildering. But she did it, that feisty little kid, not afraid of anything (except, as it would turn out to be, cockroaches).

Tommy, a grade school pal of Dea's who always wore glasses, broke his arm one day. In empathy Dea went to school with her arm in a makeshift sling and a pair of horn rimmed glasses with the glass removed.

Shortly after he broke his arm, his mother died. Dea tried to care for him emotionally. One day he ran out of the classroom crying. It was told to 'me' that Dea followed to comfort him. She had such compassion for him and other people who needed her. If she could find what you needed or had lost, she was happy and always then felt like a hero. Maybe she should have been a nurse or nun. "Oh, no."

✿ The costume shop was now in the part of the building that was once the apartment. Though big, but still not big enough, it barely worked. (I've made a deal with the lady upstairs that in my next life she must be sure to give 'me' a lot more room).

✿ Behind the theatre, a storefront became available. I walked by there one morning, saying to myself:

"Margie, this might make a better place for the costume shop. Maybe I'll move it. Maybe being on a commercial street will give us some visibility and be a smart change."

It didn't take long to scope it out, the price was right, it cost nothing to make the move, except the rent, and so that is what was unwisely, so foolishly done by 'me'. How could I know?

To say this was a miserable five years is only part of the story. My kids both said at times, "Mom, you've got to get back to the theatre. This place is changing you. You always look mad and scared, it isn't for you."

"And yep, that was the truth."

My lease was up and the move back to my safe theatre was on the boards. The former costume shop, the one we used to call "Studio B" and the part that was once the apartment, was now completely vacant and it afforded 'me' the opportunity to visualize the whole area with a new eye and fresh perspective.

A few walls were taken out, the counter moved, the floor refinished, walls painted, new electricity, new racks and shelves. Just so many things were done that would never have been seen if the change, had never been made. (Community service help did much of the physical work).

So a five-year mistake, that cost many dollars, cost time, cost nightly worries and temporarily turned Margie into a 'mad

Margie,' for sixty months, was over. In spite of all the qualms, the end result was a positive thing.

It opened my senses to the possibility that never would have been except for the seemingly ill-fated move.

The counter we use in the costume shop was once the altar of the church, and that is such a nice feeling to look at and feel good about every day.

Originally when the costume shop was just a germ of an idea in Davy's head, another mortgage was put on my building to buy him a house that was just several blocks from here.

A charming Victorian residence where Davy could live and have a business he called The Belrose Onstage Backstage Shop.

He really wanted a department store for the theatre. Well, Marin wasn't ready for one in 1978 and still isn't and may never be.

After being there a few years, it wasn't his cup of tea and that is when things turned south because of decisions that weren't thought out.

We lost his house, a grave financial slaughter that was a nightmare and the beginning of our serious financial difficulties that went south.

Davy couldn't wait to hand over the costume business to his mom, to then be moved to the lower level of the theatre.

Then his comedy store opened, and well, you know the unfortunate story.

"This is a bit redundant I know, but some things just have to be repeated, in my mind anyway, stay with 'me' on this, okay?"

When Dea spent her days at U.C.L.A., she would come home in her little brown Honda and as she drove in she would always give a loud crow, as in Peter Pan. Until that crow, the six-hour trip always made 'me' more than tense.

One day she surprised 'me'. While teaching, she came in the front door of the theatre. Seeing only a shadow:
"May I help you?" She started to cry. "It's me, Mom, your kid."

Well, we fell into each other's arms, happily sobbing and with grateful relief.

✿ She has always been one to surprise, to make things happen.

The 'me' never knew how to play and really don't very well to this day, but somehow David and I made sure our kids knew how to play, have fun, and make the most of holidays.

✿ There are numerous places in the theatre to hide Easter eggs, play badminton (which I love), ping-pong, parties, celebrations, fun and many holiday dinners with friends on a makeshift plywood table that we set up on the stage.

When those two kids of ours were in grade school, many of their friends said how lucky they were to live in a theatre that was once an old church.

Under the stage there is a lot of storage space and my young ones would take blankets, flashlights, games and food to their makeshift fort. Lots of their friends shared their unique secret hideaway.

✿ One rainy morning I drove Davy to school and reached over to kiss him goodbye. Lots of kids were running by,
"Better not kiss you with all your friends looking."
"You're my Mom and you can kiss me any time you want."

✿ A girl in Dea's second grade class asked, "What church do you go to?"

"I don't have to go to church, I live in one." As I said, "what a feisty little kid."

About the same time in history, my second grade kid said, "Mommy, there is a new girl in school and she is in my class."

"Are you making friends? Tell 'me' about her."

"Her name is Violet and her desk is next to mine. We play tetherball together at recess. I don't know her very well yet, she is still new, but she has a really nice tan, and she is funny."

Dea forgot her lunch several days later, so brought it to her. Looking in the little glass window to her classroom door, there was my child secretly whispering to Violet, the cute little child of color sitting next to her new friend, Dea. "Was I proud of her innocents and her loving nature, as I still am today? You betcha."

Davy and Dea were so close that they would protect each other no matter what. A young man who was a student here for many years got married. Davy was his best man. Another young man about Davy's age came up to me saying,

"Is your daughter here?"

"Yes, she is over there." He looked a bit nervous. "Why are you looking at her like that?"

"When we were in grade school, all of us boys were scared of her."

"How can that be? She was always such a small, wiry little girl"

"But she was tough and if anyone said anything against her brother she would attack anyway she could, usually by kicking them and then running away."

"Oh boy, was she brave, and all the fellows were afraid of her, and she wasn't afraid of anyone."

I don't think she is to this day (except cockroaches, which

we'll talk about later). Davy, in turn, was always Dea's defender, forever watching her back.

❀ When Dea finished sixth grade her teacher, Mr. Allison, gave her straight A's.
"How could I not? She wrote at least thirty book reports. What a good sweet student."

All her book reports are stored on a shelf in the prop room. Dea doesn't do much reading these days. Maybe college reading did her in.

There are many things in life we all must do and maybe even love to do and maybe even hate to do (well, you knew that).

❀ On my list of "hate to do" is vacuuming, shopping of any kind, making my bed, folding the laundry, and though cooking is not my thing, it is the clean up that is on my "hate to do" list. Oh, yes, loading and unloading the dishwasher has to be included. And now, trying to get into the technology of today, namely this **** computer.

❀ My "to do" list is extensive, overwhelming and some of it very often spills into the "hate to do list."
Maybe none of this could be much fun, but are any of these things on my "hate to do list" fun?

❀ Have a roadster, a '54 MG TF. "I love it, absolutely love it."
However, it is everything a car should not be. It is windy, loud, hot, cold, bumpy, and small and was never comfortable.

When it came into my life, used, over 30 years ago, other cars were also smaller and not so rumbling and scary.

It is no longer possible to take "Miss Sally" on the freeway now because of the big cars and how frighteningly loud they are. I can scamper around town, go to the grocery store (on my "hate to do" list)- anywhere but the freeway. I feel isolated at times. When this cute little roadster was bought in 1976 there were only 25,000 miles on its' rebuilt Volvo motor. Today it has all of 50,000 miles. "Am I a traveler?"

And speaking of traveling, it too is on my "hate to do" list. When "Miss Sally" is parked, I turn to look back at her. "What a cutie you are." Buy a big car? Can't do that.

David and I had a little yellow '68 Volkswagen convertible. My first really stupid mistake at that time was to trade it in on a small '66 Jag. That became too expensive to run so it was after that when I fell in love with the MG.

"Oh, yes, 'the me' has done some dumb, dumb things, even when things were supposedly cleverly planned."

Maybe there is a bit of Virgo in 'me', because of an obstinate compulsion to be organized (to a point). 3000 LP records all catalogued according to name of song and artist, which took years to do (with help).

All the shows we have ever done, too many to count, are all in their individual boxes, and also boxes with pictures of that show's performers.

The costumes are organized in their particular areas, although there are a few "messy corners" in the shop that terrorize 'me' daily.

There are hundreds of books, mostly autobiographies and biographies of theatre people, that with, unrelenting patience, have attempted to organize more than once. Gave up, too many, too puzzling. I'm not a librarian, but still cannot resist working on the formidable project.

❀ My closet is shamefully small, (good thing I'm not a clothes horse) and there is no possibility that it can ever be called a closet or can ever be right in anyone's eyes.

❀ "Hmmm how about the things that haven't been touched in years?" I'll get to them (that's a promise) and do the right thing. (I think)."

❀ In my earlier days (oh, dear, when was that?) Ah, yes, when my kids were young, everything was kept clean and orderly. But now since I'm alone, in looking around, gasping: "Really need to clean out the fridge. Gosh, could fix that up, should paint that, and maybe move that to a better place. Could scrub my bathroom and kitchen. Why are all those clothes on the floor and hung over anything and everything? And where does all that dust come from? Why not put away some of the books piled everywhere?

Why is that paint bucket still in the corner of my small kitchen, after a year?"

However most things get done that shriek for attention to be taken care of every day. You see:

❀ The energy is that I am caught up in keeping the theatre and shop almost tiptop. I fail in this regard sometimes too. Then when my hectic day is over and taking a slow and exhausted walk into my humble abode, which is in the back of the theatre, oh dear, my little home takes second place. (No, probably no place at all).

But I'll tell you, whatever was done right in this area when my two adults were two adorable, young babes in the woods, have made them both into ghastly "clean freaks."

"Gosh, wish they would come over and do their ghastly things here that they do so well there."

One night a few years ago, impulsively jumping out of bed because of being uncontrollably inspired, I grabbed paper and pencil and started to write as quickly as possible lyrics to a song and then another and another to over 31 songs (or poems if you will). "No, no, this didn't all happen in that one highly stimulated night."

I have even been able to get the music down to some of the lyrics, with the help of a musician or two, as this Margie is not one. "How did this happen? Where did the words come from? I don't know. Will never know."

Now have bumped into an acute dry spell. But, no matter, if all these lyrics get music, and they get out there that will be enough. That will be satisfying; that will be an artistic accomplishment never dreamed of.

In time we'll see what comes of this creative explosion. "Could be good, could be put in a drawer to gather some of the dust that hangs around, maybe they will all have to wait for another day to come into their own." All of the songs are copyrighted and some lyrics are included in this story.

"Thank you my new and considerate lawyer friend, Bob Gordon, for unselfishly taking on what seems to me, a mammoth undertaking, that of having all of them copyrighted. "Hmm, maybe I'll be rich and famous. If so, will share, promise."

My two charges were not always the wonderful people that they were at one time and now again. During the terrible eighties, after the financial closure of the comedy club, they both did dumb, stupid things. (Oh, yes, the same for 'me').

Defeated Davy could not even look 'me' in the face, because of the guilt that surrounded him so utterly and completely, consequently he was not nice at times.

He slept all day, barely crawled out of bed just in time to help with cleaning offices, and then off to his bartending job. This was his near destructive pattern for many months.

Very early one three a.m. morning, still having to get up by seven to clean a house or two, he woke 'me' up, tearful; "Is something terrible happening?"

But, thank God, no. He had gone into a storage area and began looking through a box that was boldly marked: "The Changing of a Man, David Belrose"

Why he would do that so early in the morning, he does not know. But his mumbling words to the sleepy 'me' were, "I can do better than Dad, can't I? Dad really messed up, didn't he?" (I don't believe he said messed). "Yes, you can, and you better. Children should do better than their parents. That is evolution."

That revealing early dawn conversation changed Davy's life. From then on most everything for him has been positive and he again became my loving, my productive son.

"He was now healthy and happy, a part of him that was missing for so long."

I had to call Dea in Los Angeles, asking, near begging her, to come home and help save our beautiful building, our home, and 'me'.

She had plans, tentative plans, to maybe try her hand, well, actually, her feet, in New York.

She selflessly and quickly put all that aside and came to my rescue. Of course she was resentful of Davy and 'me' too, for this unexpected turn of events, and was not, for a while, the sweet person she had always been.

But when all was said and done, she too became my very kind and loving daughter once more. Funny and happy. The nightmare was over, but her dream to travel to the big apple scene, will never be.

"I am so sorry, my daughter, I still grieve today. Please forgive 'me': please forgive that most terrible of times we all suffered through. No one's fault, really. Just unwise decisions and mistakes that we didn't know would drastically change our lives."

The guilt that will forever and ever be felt by 'me' is that Dea was asked to come home to help.

"Would she have gone to New York? Who is to know?" Show business is so tentative, so fragile, so unkind, so wicked and unforgiving, so ruthless, careless, so tirelessly demanding in every way. And then, poof, it is over only too quickly.

"Who do you know? Who can you trust? Will you be at the right place at the right time, with the talent needed? Will my little and sensitive Dea be strong enough emotionally to find her way in such a mad, selfish, jealous, uncaring jungle?"

She did manage to successfully scramble thru four years of college and to graduate from U.C.L.A., so YES she could have.

"I did not know what else to do, could have just laid down and drowned in the cold numbness that enclosed 'me' every minute of every day for so long. But that wasn't in 'me' to do. Needed help from her and others, asked for it, and it came."

✿ We three were suffering in countless ways at that dreadful time in our changing lives from unbelievable tension, fears, overwork, and stress. And it showed in our behavior towards one another.

"My God, how did we get through it? How did we remain friends and become a loving family again?"

But like most things, time took care of us three, very scared Belrose family, through sacrifice, perseverance, and certainly our love and respect for one another and what we had. Now here we are continuing to always take care of one another, with all the loving kindness we have in our bodies and souls.

✿ Damn, I always meant to keep a diary/journal…never did…life was then and is now too hectic and by the time beddy-bye time comes I just want to vegetate. There were times actually did keep a sort of journal, but only now and then.

There are so many cute and precious and not so precious times here with the pupils and performers, in my school and theatre.

✿ For instance, a little girl, Terry, about six years old, her two front teeth were knocked out. She was asked to do a step across the floor. There was a pole in front of her (now gone). She said in her cute way with her teeth missing "Mithy Margie, the pole is in my way."

"Terry, since the pole can't be moved, maybe you will have to." Of course, you would have had to be there to appreciate the innocence of such a sweet scene.

❁ Another time, six-year-old Debbie was taking a pre-ballet class. As she was being taught to stand in second position, she opened her legs and went tinkle. I looked at the other children with a menacing look to indicate "Do not laugh," I quickly took Debbie into my apartment where she put on a pair of Dea's panties. We came back to the class and went on with the lesson as if nothing ever happened. Another moment never to be forgotten, and probably not by her either, even today.

❁ Speaking of ballet, it was lovingly taught by 'me' for years to both young children and adults, cherished it with all my heart. But now there is an incomprehensible amount of competition out in our complicated and diversified world, not just in dance: soccer gets in the way, as do other non-dance activities.

I just can't fight the loose-loose battle anymore, but will always miss repeating those beautiful French words and the discipline of my first love.

❁ The tiny tots taking classes were always something I looked forward to. Now at this time of my life, no, I don't want to crawl on the floor to demonstrate frog jumps, crab walks, cartwheels, or spider walks. "Those days are sadly gone. Are they missed and were they loved? A big YES!"

Teaching an absolutely inspiring and creative acting class of children around twelve to fourteen years, one afternoon they were each asked to demonstrate what their mothers, fathers or teachers did when they were angry. After this hilarious and yet touching exercise was over, talented Diana said, "I think someone should show Miss Margie what she looks like when she is angry."

"Okay, Diana, you show us." Standing up, she put her left hand on her waist, pointed her right finger at everyone, gently stamped her right foot and said, "Now, you have not been the best kind of people you can be."

Not another thing was said and the class continued. And that was it. Guess you would had to be there also to appreciate this extraordinary moment in time and my career. Diana is still my dear friend and is just now turning fifty. She came to both our fifty and fifty-fifth anniversaries. She remembers it all.

While cleaning the home of some rather wealthy people (during those terrible eighties), one morning saw a note on the fridge that said: "Don't 'should' me."

It was meant for her husband, of course. But, loving that expression, my concerted effort has since been to never "should" anyone. Instead I have said, "May I suggest? How do you feel about doing it this way?" and such, but never 'should'. I have wondered if her husband took it to heart.

Gosh, there are so many stories. Was it Jimmy Durante who said, "I've got a million of 'em?"

❀ I have some stories that are not so precious, touching or cute, but need to be forgotten and forgiven. Some performers and students with egos and attitudes would send 'me' into tears at the end of the teaching or rehearsal day. Things that were said and done, many did hurt 'me', but more importantly, most have taught 'me'.

To even touch further on hundreds of delightful anecdotes would make this book about 5000 pages.

"Nope, can't do that to you or to 'me'.

❀ My children have forbidden 'me' to ever go to a county fair alone again. (It's never any fun anyway). But in 1991 and 1992 respectively the fair found 'me' wondering and looking.

In '91 there was a Softub gently teasing 'me'. Always wanted such a decadent tub. It wasn't too expensive and can even be used inside. It is light enough to carry, without water, of course. I no longer have a bathtub, and I love to soak, so I bought it.

❀ There is a flat roof in the back of the theatre, used to have pull-down steps to get up there. "Something must be done with this space."

In '92 going to the fair (alone again) there was a greenhouse that was staring 'me' in the face, deliciously enticing 'the me' "It would be great to put me up on your roof." I went furtively to the Planning Department asking if it would be possible. I truly, truly did not think it could happen, but was immediately told: "Yes, you can, your building is already three stories high."

Sooooo, called the green house people, plus a contractor friend of mine, and by November of '92, there it was. It is my glass house, my bedroom and my favorite hideaway "Oh, yes, this was one of the small refinances."

✿ "Has this very seldom impetuous person been to the fair again alone? Nope." I am not a compulsive buyer. In fact, I am not a buyer at all, but these two things had to be. "You can see that, can't you?" I promised myself was not going to talk about the glass house, but a special pupil, Michelle, in a most inspiring tap class, said, "Margie, you have to tell about this. It is wonderful, and I want to see your glass house."

"When my apartment is shiny and clean, (that will be the day), including the glass house, then you'll all be invited to see my special place. Has it all been said? Don't know" Maybe in my next book. Well, maybe not. Just a few more tidbits, if you could indulge 'me' a bit more.

✿ Dea went off to U.C.L.A. and we found a darling small apartment, painted it, put rugs on the floor, made curtains to match the bed covers, painted second-hand furniture, and even got a front doorknob to match.

It all seemed perfect. Although the apartment was in a somewhat depressed area, a complex of about ten apartments, we felt it was safe. Less than a month later she called,

"Mom, I can't live here any more. The cockroaches from other apartments come out at night and all I hear is their dropping to the floor, to the counter, to the shelves. I can't even get up to go to the bathroom for fear of stepping on them. I'm sorry, Mom, I know we fixed this up so special, but just can't live here any longer, got to move right away."

And she did. So you see this feisty kid of mine had more than met her match – cockroaches.

When David could no longer set foot on this earth, it was important for 'me' to reorganize the apartment, to change everything, even the furniture.

Dea and Davy were thirteen and fifteen, so I bought captain's furniture and moved each into other rooms to give them a fresh outlook also.

(These rooms are now what are called The Prop Shop).

I began to paint the apartment walls, shingling some of them. My world, temporarily, did indeed look like a war zone as a friend at the time said.

Davy walked in one day after school when I had a hammer in my hand. "Mom, I've got to talk to you. Please put down the hammer." This had to be serious, so putting down the possibly threatening hammer, and sitting among the chaotic pandemonium, I listened.

"Mom, Kathy wants to make love; she's done it before. She's had lots of boyfriends."

Kathy was a freshman in college and one of my dance students, Davy just a freshman in high school. So with motherly wisdom: "Well, Davy, do you want to?"

"If I do, then I have to really care about her. I have to see her all the time, take her out, buy her gifts, tell her I love her, call often, and, Mom, I just don't think I am ready for all that. I'm just a kid."

"Davy, if you did would you know what to do?"

"Not really, but why don't you tell me what you know."

About six months later, my growing up Davy, said out of the bright blue sky: "Bet you wonder if I am still going with Kathy and doing what she wants? I wasn't ready then, but I sure am now."

The inevitable passage of my young son's innocence.

🌼 When Dea and Davy were quite young they did a few years of modeling for Scott lawn products, Ford Car Company, Jantzen swimwear, etc., but the biggie for Dea was doing the chocolate box for Ghirardelli Chocolate Company.

The picture of her cute face and a young male model were on opposite sides of the box. One day while meandering about at Ghirardelli Square, Dea scanned the display of boxes to find that they were almost all turned so the other model's picture was showing. She very cleverly turned most of the boxes so her picture would be seen and not that many of the other young model.

As said, "what a feisty kid." (Just remembered the 'me' also did a print ad for "Rid' insect" hmmm about 100 years ago, which is not too far off).

🌼 We used to have a treasured, tiny painted metal box in our family called "the surprise box" when the kids were in grade school.

They would come running home to find the box and then to see what was in it. Sometimes something, other times nothing, other times money, sometimes sent them on a wild goose chase. It was an exciting and eager game for them. They now share yearly ownership of the box, in their respective homes, to this day.

Please don't think I don't like animals. "I do, I do."
And this will be of interest to only those that do.

🌼 We had two poodle mix females, one for Davy and one for Dea. Suzette, an out-of-control dog, ran off early one school morning, to at least four or five blocks. Was hit by a car.

Her sister, Nanette, a more docile dog, became my dog for some reason. She lived a wonderful nineteen years.

Then a string of female cats came into our lives:

- Pearly Mae, a beautiful white shorthaired Persian, lived to about fifteen years. Then another gray shorthaired Persian, Big Mamma, had her for about three years, and then someone ran away with her.

- Skitters, a black and white mix – and she was just what her name implied. She skittered around, and we had her for about fifteen years.

- Now, mind you, many of these animals overlapped each other. Sometimes it was certain we were living in a small zoo, with bunnies, hamsters, fish, birds, besides the cats and dogs.

  When all the animals were gone, I wanted, no needed, a little dog by this time and purchased a black (that eventually turned gray) teacup poodle.

- Docile and sweet, Rosie was loved by everyone. That adorable thing was nine years old when she unexpectedly came onto the stage and a set piece that was being moved fell on her. Without even a whimper, she was gone from my life.

- My current dog, Binky, is an apricot-colored teacup poodle that will lick you silly if you let her. Loving, rambunctious and adorable. She turned six years old as of March 2010.

  This is the end of my animal stories. Will there be another animal in my world once dear Binky goes to animal heaven? Don't really know.

  The dogs and cats in my life have been precious to have, play with, and to share my bed. When a person has had absolutely great animals in their life: they just can't do better. "Well maybe a horse next time around, or a pink polka dot elephant."

✿ Dea took French starting in the seventh grade. She didn't
do well with it, even when with a tutor. One lunchtime, as a
sophomore, she called:

"Mom, why am I taking French? "

"Because I couldn't and you are going to."

"Oh, just wanted to know." This foreign language helped her
to be accepted into U.C.L.A..

✿ This was the same child that at three years old strutted into
the kitchen one summer morning. Her fingers were in the
waistband of her little jeans.

"What would you like for breakfast, Dea?"

"My name's not Dea. My name's Sam."

She moseyed around in her cowboy character all day (guess
she was already an actress). The next morning the same question
was answered:

"I'm not Sam today Mom, I'm Dea."

"Welcome home my little Dea."

To this day every card or note from my Dea to 'me' is signed
"Sam'.

One last little tidbit.:

✿ Dea came home one Saturday with a first place sweater patch
she won for winning a 'yo yo' contest.

"Dea I've never seen you with a yo yo. How did you win?"

"I was the only person in my age group that showed up, so I
won." Sounds like an old vaudeville joke, doesn't it?

TO CONTINUE WITH TIDBITS

I have to now highlight famous or near famous people I knew, barely knew, they've been here or have touched my life ever so lightly for a brief moment in time. (Not in any particular order).

- Barbara Hale, who played Perry Mason's secretary Della Street. She came to check out the Belrose for her teen-age daughter's jazz classes. We talked a few minutes.

- William Windom, who portrayed the doctor on "Murder She Wrote." He did two one-man shows here. He had been a terrific actor, performing many roles during his long and distinguished career.

- My daughter flew in from Los Angeles to see Gene Kelly's one-man show. In driving her back to the Airporter, she said,

   "I wonder how Mr. Kelly will get home?"

   "He probably will catch a plane, just like you are doing." Walking down the aisle of the plane, there sat Gene Kelly. She breathlessly said,

   "Oh, Mr. Kelly, I just saw your show. What are you doing here?"

   "Well, I have to get home, too. (Noticing her tap shoes deliberating hanging out of her over stuffed bag,) Are you a tapper?" They talked for a few minutes, then after landing she ran around to where she knew he would be. They walked together to her very cluttered college girl Honda and they said good night. "Nice, don't you think?"

❀ A little girl came into the studio one early afternoon.
"My Mommie says you are famous."
"Oh, not really,"
"I know you are famous."
"Here at 1415 Fifth Avenue I am." (She stamped her foot).
"No my Mommie says you're famous."
"OK, your right, I'm famous."
That was that. Later it dawned on 'me'. She just wanted to meet a famous person…no matter who that personage might be.

❀ I became a good friend of Keefe Brasselle. He played Eddie Cantor in the film The Eddie Cantor Story, as well as being in many movies and doing a television variety show. He was a sweet man and fell fatherly in love with young Dea.
A few days before he passed away he called, "Margie, I need you to come to Los Angeles right away."
"Can't do that, Keefe, am in a show."
He became angry and hung up. A few days later he died. "Was a show worth that 'No'?"

❀ Tommy Tune and his friend came into the costume shop. He rented a simple but very nice Dracula cape. His partner chose a fancy pirate costume.

❀ Marge and Gower Champion were doing a show in San Francisco. On their closing night, my friends Paul and Ethel O'Brien (of the Capezio Store) had a late chili supper for them. We two Belroses, were invited to the small gathering.
Sat next to Marge. We talked a little and she promised to send me an autographed picture, and did. It hung in my reception area for many years. One day it was gone. "I hope that thief is enjoying my treasured picture as much as I did all those years."

❀ About the same time had met Ruth St. Dennis, backstage, a very famous dancer in her day. She also sent 'me' an autographed picture of herself, and it too was taken the same time the picture of the Champion's was discovered stolen. Karma people.

❀ Ronn Lucas, the fabulous ventriloquist, (he had performed in Davy's comedy club) came into the theatre.

"Gosh, you look just like Ronn Lucas."

"I am Ronn Lucas." (This was during the terrible eighties). He walked 'me' to his darling little apartment, not far from the Belrose. Taking out his checkbook he wrote one to 'me' for $1,000, just like that. He has had a very successful career. Keep thinking one day he just might walk in again and I'll say "Gosh you look just like Ronn Lucas."

❀ Frank Olivea, an incredible juggler on a one-wheel bike, yet, very inventive. He performed with Ronn Lucas, Ann Miller and Mickey Rooney in Sugar Babes. Went backstage to again meet him. He also performed here at The Belrose and in Davy's Flatiron Comedy Club.

❀ Patti Colombo, now a well-known choreographer, was my young talented student here for at least seven years. She went on to bigger and better things (as she should have), established a reputation for herself in the world of theatre. Among many achievements in her career, as far as I know, she choreographed the last Broadway production of Peter Pan.

Saw her father one Father's Day in a restaurant a few years ago. He walked over to my table and secretly said, "We know where Patti started and got her early training. Thank you, Miss Margie."

❀ Met and became good friends, with Katie Heflin, the daughter of the late movie star Van Heflin. She is a lover of horses and I believe she lives in West Marin with her horses. We've lost touch.

✤ Years ago a Mr. Ivan Morrison signed up his little girl for a tiny tot class. On the registration card he wrote as his occupation "composer-singer/performer."

   "Are you able to make a living as an entertainer?"

   Very shyly he said, "Well, I'm known as Van Morrison." Oops! Let's see who else has been here (can't remember them all).

✤ Robin Williams (before he became THE Robin Williams) did a five-minute act down center stage for five dollars, later performed often in Davy's Comedy Club. Saw him many times at the yearly Comedy Day Celebration in Golden Gate Park. He was always truly nice to Davy and 'the me'.

✤ Ducks Breath performed here several times, as well as Will Durst, Mike Pritchard, the late Jose Simon, several improvisation groups: SOS, Papaya Juice. The fabulous Meehan Brothers, Diane Amos (the Pine Sol lady).

✤ The well-known writer (of many years ago) Peggy Bracken had a driver bring her two young children for Saturday morning classes.

✤ Bob Gordon, a beloved (by everyone) show biz attorney, and you may not even know he is also starting his own performing career.

✤ Herb Eiseman who headed the B.M.I. office in Los Angeles. Still my friend. He helped my late husband, David, in the sixties, when David was writing so profusely and had great dreams.

✤ Bill Cunningham, a highly respected and well-known agent, with offices in Los Angeles and New York (now retired). He has been a long-time friend of mine, and in fact we took tap lessons together with Mr. Kahn, oh,

   "Let's see, maybe a hundred years ago. Nah, it couldn't be that long ago."

✤ The fabulous classy tap and comedy trio, The Dunhill's. Jerry Kurland of the Dunhill's taught a few classes here as well as working with Dea privately. Jerry has had a long and successful career in Hollywood, Vegas and New York. As far as I know he is still 'doing his thing' on stage.

❁ I was fortunate to be invited into Chita Rivera's dressing room at The Venetian room with my friend Rick Dolph. He knew her at one time and then they became reacquainted after her show when she herself, incredibly, invited us to visit in her dressing room.

❁ Harold Lang, a Broadway song and dance performer and I believe the second Pal Joey on Broadway after Gene Kelly. He came into my theatre, over thirty- five years ago, with my friend Lynn. He planned on doing a show here, but became ill and died shortly after our brief meeting.

❁ Francis Swann, a well-known Hollywood writer, wrote "Out of the Frying Pan," (the most produced play in the country, of its' day, from the Samuel French catalogue of plays) it became a movie with William Holden. He was a prolific writer of plays and novels, for many years. He is the man who introduced 'me' and Dea to Keefe Brasselle.

We produced a play of his and then a plan was set in motion for him to write another for The Belrose. Before that project could get under way, he passed from this world.

❁ His sister, Lynn Swann Keller, was the actress/director who encouraged me to do "Peter Pan." We remained friends until her death in her early nineties.

❁ I met and knew a lot of the comedians of the seventies and eighties, the late Jose Simon, being one of them, who headed the Comedy Day Celebration in Golden Gate Park for many successful and funny years. It was thrilling and fun to be the yearly timekeeper, along with Davy and Damien as the stage managers.

❁ Wrote a fan letter to Ginger Rogers when I was an impressionable young girl, and still am, well not a young girl, but have always remained impressionable. She responded with a post card, which is of course with my valued yellowed treasures.

❀ Wrote two fan letters to Donald O'Connor when he was quite ill, and then another when he recovered. He sent me his autographed picture, which proudly hangs on my personal wall of pictures. This not long before he became ill again and said goodbye to the world that he displayed his incredible talent to. I attended his one-man show, and he was MARVELOUS as always. He performed full out, not holding back.

❀ The King Sisters, after they recorded David's "Who Would Remember" were performing in the Fairmont's Venetian Room. They came to David's and my table and privately sang his song to us. My friend Sue Sue arranged this special time.

❀ Knew very well, Bill Howell, a dancer with the Denis-Shawn Dancers of the forties, who later became an important TV. Director of 'soaps' in New York.

❀ Worked with an old time Vaudevillian tap dancer, Eddie Brown. For many weeks, he would manage to get on a bus from San Francisco to San Rafael to give both Dea and I a very professional and inspiring master tap lesson, till he had to move away. He was a delightful curmudgeon.

❀ When as a wide-eyed eighteen year old, mesmerized by 'show biz', I was in a small show and the guest performer for several nights, was the screen's siren, Yvonne DeCarlo. Don't remember what she did or what we said to each other, what the show was about, or what this inexperienced Margie person did. I just know I was chomping at the bit to move to San Francisco and really get down in the trenches to study dance. Gosh, if I have forgotten you or anyone, please forgive 'me'.

Gotsa bitty bit more to tell about > > > > > > >

WHAT IF, WHAT IF, WHAT IF

Any one, just one, of these things or people could have changed my life drastically and taken 'me' quite possibly in another direction.

(Not in any order).

- Sister Theresa had not been so kind to me.

- When in Huntington, West Virginia, Dorcus Holt had adopted me.

- My father would have left me with my Thea in New Jersey.

- I went to Sacramento that night and not Lodi.

- I never put the ad in the paper and then met the Ferrone family to take care of and love me.

- I never met the Papalias family who befriended me for years.

- I never met Paul and Ethel O'Brien who so wisely guided me to the right professional teachers.

- Stanley and Pat Kahn did not let me teach for them all the while training 'me'.

- I never met David Belrose, to be enamored of him, and who enriched my life, and was my true-life teacher.

- I never met the Abrams family to unselfishly help us buy this building that gave Margie and David an extraordinary life. They believed in us. What if I didn't have the nerve to ask them for help?

- I never knew Norma who was my forever friend and paid off our last humongous mortgage. "How could she know what this great gift to 'me' would do?"

- I never met Wilfred George who contributed to this place called the Belrose and paid off our first mortgage and other things. I thank him so much. I miss him.

- I never fell passionately in love with dance at three years old.

- I never saw this vacant church and the guidance of George Steinert.

- My Papa was a good and honest man, a real father, and a person I could trust and love.

- I had never met Damien who helped the theatre grow in many ways, but then abandoned 'me' and this theatre he called "his stage."

- I never had my two exceptional children to love and cherish, to teach me and to love me back.

- I never went to Lodi High.

- I never had the chance to teach and perform.

- I did not know the loyalty that Sue Sue gave me and mine.

- I never acquired the many true friends I have, maybe even you, who are reading this book.

- I never met and knew my talented and creative Davida as my student, friend, inspiration, and now my teacher.

- My mother did not abandon my sister and 'me' and if she had been a good unselfish person to know and love.

- I did not know what "not" to be.

- I picked that one number to win the lottery so I could help all my friends and even an enemy or two.

"Is our world made up of WHAT IFS?
Perhaps some of your what ifs have or will come true."

To seek out the many forgotten or pushed back memories has been a surreal experience for 'me', which often became too painful to relive or share.

However they were and are the substance and essence of my life. In writing down these thousands of words it also became necessary to leave out some of those remembrances.

In the final analysis, these many remembered scenes shared with you within these pages, and other memories, that need to be boxed away, with no title roughly scratched on such a box, they total up to the raggedy fabric that has made up my bumpy journey into.

THE ME I FOUND
Oh, our stroll is not quite finished.

Stay with me for a few more pages. > > > > >

GOOD GRIEF, IS THIS ANOTHER ENDING? Yep.

"How could I forget to tell you of my performing life? "
It has been one of the most important elements of my adult years,
my time of creativity and personal growth.

"Let's forget the sad young years, deal?"

"What to do when David died?"

🌼 He wrote and directed all of our shows. One being a darling
play, Country Dumplins. Loved playing a crabby Grandma
Trouble. Was too much fun. In fact, we produced the play three
more times (two after his death;) it was that good and so funny.

"Then again, what to do next? " In talking to a director/actress
friend of mine:

"Lynn always wanted to perform Peter Pan."

"Then do it." "Don't think I have it in me, can't."

"Why not. This is your place and you can do anything
you want, good or bad, take your chances."

🌼 Therefore with more bravery than thought possible in 'me',
performed in two separate productions of Peter Pan.

"Then, what do you think?"

🌼 Had the guts to produce, direct, and perform, and partially write
dozens of vaudeville and revue shows thru the years.

🌼 The Miracle Worker will always be a major thrill just to
remember working with Dea as Helen Keller, myself as Annie
Sullivan, and receiving two unexpected positive reviews.

- The Lion in Winter, playing Queen Eleanore with 600 lines to deliver for eight different years and three of those with Davy playing Richard the Lion Heart.

  "Would you say this is just about my favorite play?"

  (With 600 lines to deliver, I know I am not suffering from a mental decline).

- Two separate years of Dial M for Murder turned out well.

- My own one-woman show, Stuff Happens, followed several years later with, Wait Till You Hear What I've Got To Say. And more recently, Tidbits. We have done dozens of original plays.

- Loved, just loved playing Abby in Arsenic and Old Lace for two separate years. One of my favorites.

- The Mad Woman of Chaillot was clearly an artistic success. It was a challenge and loved it.

- The Big Knife was a scary project to direct and produce. It was an artistic success also.

- With much gusto and fun played the Wicked Witch in The Wizard of Oz. (There is no doubt, that she was fashioned after Sister Mary Matthew. Why in the world would I choose to play that part? Don't know, maybe to get back at her, ha!).

- Oh, God, we did so many versions of A Christmas Carol. Too much work, too many performers, can never do it again.

- At least a dozen original audience participation murder mysteries were always successful, some of them cleverly written by Damien.

- He also wrote an original spoof on Marin County. We both collaborated on and named it "Hello Marin Hello."

  This highly successful play ran for thirteen consecutive months and could have run longer but for the cast that needed to make changes in their lives. I think this play is what turned The

Belrose into a near professional theatre. It was good for us. Maybe I'll revamp it and do it again.

- Playing Nancy in Oliver was also something to live up to, as was my being the producer, choreographer, and one of the directors.

- In searching for 'the me' I discovered along this creative path of mine that certain kinds of clowns capture my heart. Consequently I acquired a small collection of them. 'Me' has a quiet clown deep inside that needs to experience the world. This tender tramp clown of mine, is not an overly made up one, not much of a silly one, not a scary one, but a clown that has pathos, seeming at first like a looser only to shine forth as the hero. My tramp clown's name is Binker and we have done lots of shows together. Binker has freed me enough to expand into another imaginative part of the performing 'me'. Binker makes me happy and we understand each other.

- I started a Thursday nite open mic over sixteen years ago as suggested by singers Stephanie Hendricks and Dore Green. It has been a weekly event. Many people have partially centered their lives on it. 'The me' certainly does. I get to sing every week, often doing my own 'stuff."

In forty- eight years there are just too many to name any more. "But you probably have gotten the idea of this very important part of my life. Right?"
"So has this Margie person really come to the end of strolling hand in hand with you on this lazy daisy day, through my bumpy journey of life?"
Performing so many parts in countless plays has undeniably been, in large measure, responsible for …

THE ME I FOUND,
While discovering and believing
"Life is Just a Bowl of Cherries"

Thank you. You've been patient strolling with me hand in hand
thru my ventures, so attentive, and I love you more.
Our journey together has almost come to a gentle end.

A sense of sweetness and quiet surround
THE ME I FOUND.

WHO AM I

Lyrics by Margie Belrose

Dedicated to the loving clown in all of us

WHO AM I? I'VE GOT A SMILE IN MY HEART,
BUT WHO AM I?
I'VE GOT A SMILE ON MY FACE, BUT WHO AM I?
MY SOUL IS FILLED WITH JOY AS I TRY EACH DAY
TO KEEP PACE
I LOOK FOR THE GOODNESS, MAYBE EVEN
IN YOUR FACE
SWEETNESS FILLS THE AIR
AND I SHALL TRY EACH AND EVERY DAY
TO NOT HAVE A CARE
BUT WHO AM I?
THAT FACE IN THE CLOUDS?
I WONDERED WHO COULD THAT ONE BE
I KNOW IT'S ME, A CLOWN, A FUNNY HAPPY CLOWN
OR IS IT JUST A DREAM, ANOTHER OF
MY SILLY DREAMS
NO, IT IS ME, A FUNNY CLOWN
WITH A SMILE IN MY HEART
AND JOY IN MY SOUL
WHO AM I? AT LAST I KNOW, JUST A FUNNY CLOWN
THE ME I FOUND

THE SOUND OF QUIET

Lyrics by Margie Belrose Music by Alan Young
Dedicated that each quiet morning continues to greet me

THE SOUND OF QUIET COMES
BEFORE THE OPENING OF SPRING
WHEN BIRDS WILL ALWAYS SING
AND THE RIVERS WILL REACH GENTLY
FOR THEIR SHORES
THE SOUND OF QUIET IS ALL AROUND
AND WE MUST LISTEN AS IT GIVES OUR SENSES
TIME TO HEAR THE QUIET OF EACH SOUND
THAT TOUCHES THE CENTER OF OUR SOULS
IN AN ALMOST SACRED AND QUIET WAY
WHEN THE TROUBLES OF THE DAY COME UPON US
GO GENTLE, BE QUIET AND
THE ANSWERS WILL COME OUR WAY
FOR WE MUST LISTEN FOR THE QUIET AGAIN
AND AGAIN
SO THAT WE MAY HEAR THE
OPENING OF SPRING WHEN BIRDS
WILL ALWAYS SING
AND THE RIVERS WILL REACH
GENTLY FOR THEIR SHORES
THE SOUND OF QUIET IS ALL AROUND
IN THE DARK OF THE NIGHT AND
AS THE DAWN AWAKENS
AND WE MUST LISTEN AS IT GIVES OUR SENSES
TIME TO HEAR THE QUIET OF EACH SOUND
THAT TOUCHES THE CENTER OF OUR SOULS IN
AN ALMOST SACRED AND QUIET WAY

© 2009 Margie Belrose

HAVE YOU NOTICED
Lyrics by Margie Belrose
Music by Jim Shelburne
Dedicated to the beauty of our ever changing world

HAVE YOU NOTICED THAT WINTER PASSES WITH THE RAIN
SNOW AND COLD ALL GONE FOR NOW
THEN SPRING BURSTS FORTH WITH ITS PROMISE OF
WARM AND LONGER DAYS
AND NATURE BEGINS TO BLOOM AND CREATURES
COME OUT OF THEIR WEEKS OF SLEEPINESS AND LETHARGY
HAPPY FACES ON ALL THE CHILDREN AS THEY SKIP, LAUGH
AND WAIT IMPATIENTLY FOR THE DAYS THAT WILL BRING
SWIMMING, HIKING, AND BEING WARMED BY THE
MARVELOUS SUN
THEN WITH HARDLY A WINK, FALL RUSHES IN WITH
UNABASHED DAYS OF BEAUTY EVERYWHERE,
CHILLY EVENINGS AND FIREPLACES
GIVING OFF WARMTH AND THE PROMISE OF
CANDLELIGHT NIGHTS
AND EVEN ROMANCE FOR SOME, IN BETWEEN
THE DIM LIT LIGHTS
OH, HOW WONDERFUL TO HAVE THE BEAUTY OF
FOUR SEASONS
EACH GIVING UNSELFISHLY THE MIRACLE OF SUCH AN
EVER CHANGING WORLD
THAT STARTS OVER AGAIN WITH WINTER
UNPREDICTABLE IN ALL ITS BEAUTY THAT WILL CHANGE FROM
ONE KIND OF BEAUTY TO ANOTHER AND ANOTHER
FOR ALL TIME TO COME

And now with this giant energetic project gloriously behind
'the me',
How many years, maybe three years, in the writing,
ten or more years in the thinking, planning, research.
And now looking to more months
to get this in its' published form.
Which is what you have been strolling thru with 'me'
But for the immediate few months I can at least plan on
cleaning that shower, and maybe
a few other nooks and crannies
I said 'plan"
Remember have yet to learn how to unring the bell,
(as told to you Charlie)
so don't know what can realistically be accomplished
but my heart is in the right place
THANK YOU
And don't you just love these curly cues
Have I overdone them?